The News Media,
Civil War, and
Humanitarian Action

The News Media, Civil War, and Humanitarian Action

Larry Minear,
Colin Scott,
Thomas G. Weiss

LYNNE
RIENNER
PUBLISHERS

BOULDER
LONDON

Published in the United States of America in 1996 by
Lynne Rienner Publishers, Inc.
1800 30th Street, Boulder, Colorado 80301

and in the United Kingdom by
Lynne Rienner Publishers, Inc.
3 Henrietta Street, Covent Garden, London WC2E 8LU

Library of Congress Cataloging-in-Publication Data
Minear, Larry, 1938–
    The news media, civil war, and humanitarian action / Larry Minear,
Colin Scott, and Thomas G. Weiss.
        p.   cm.
    Includes bibliographical references and index.
    ISBN 1-55587-662-5 (hardcover : alk. paper)
    ISBN 1-55587-676-5 (pbk. : alk. paper)
    1. War in the press. 2. Civil war. 3. Humanitarianism.
I. Scott, Colin. II. Weiss, Thomas George. III. Title.
PN4784.W37M56   1996
070.4'4935502—dc20   96-17327
                                                                CIP

British Cataloguing-in-Publication Data
A Cataloguing-in-Publication record for this book
is available from the British Library.

Printed and bound in the United States of America

        The paper used in this publication meets the requirements
 ∞ of the American National Standard for Permanence of
        Paper for Printed Library Materials Z39.48-1984.

    5 4 3 2 1

Contents

Figures and Tables

FIGURES

TABLES

Foreword

As with the tree falling in the forest, if a voice—a people—cries out for aid and there is no camera there to record it, is the need any less? Or more?

The cameras, the microphones, the reporters have recorded the plight of Somalis, Rwandans, Liberians, Bosnians, and Haitians just in the past few years. When the media come, they sometimes find humanitarian organizations already in place—caring, coping, but perhaps also crying out for help beyond their means. Those who can deliver, governments mostly, are most often moved by policy. They can, though, be compelled to move by pain and suffering faces delivered electronically to our comfortable homes from others' distant disheveled homelands.

The News Media, Civil War, and Humanitarian Action is a study of how these three sides of a triangle—media, governments, and humanitarian organizations—are reconfiguring in a changing world to address these problems. The relationships are evolving, as is the post–Cold War world.

News organizations are capable of landing small armies of reporters, producers, photographers, and technicians in remote areas with arsenals of communications equipment providing instant access to their typesetting computers and broadcast control rooms. Collectively they are a Cyclops, a giant that cannot be ignored. Television especially, with its single focused eye, commands attention. For brief but intense periods of time, the media send monocular burning images onto the screens we all watch. Scorched villages in Bosnia. Chopped bodies in Rwanda. A soldier dragged through Somali streets. Some call compelling stories that propel governments into action the *CNN factor.* Perhaps that's valid, whether the source is CNN or some other. But for all their ability to focus similarly on such stories, the media are not monolithic. And not entirely dependable. Not every tribe's tragedy is recorded.

Who will come? At first, probably a freelancer, an itinerant magazine reporter, a lone photographer. Then, perhaps, everyone.

When? Too soon, sometimes, before anyone cares. Some saw Rwanda before the bloodbath. Too late, sometimes; many saw it after. The media are rarely the first on the scene and almost never the last. Cyclops' eye swings slowly, and once it focuses somewhere else it is not easy to draw it back.

What attracts? Plight and might. No matter how desperate the indigenous situation, the story gets better when the troops arrive.

The symbiosis is great: Humanitarian organizations can use the media effectively to explain a problem and solicit aid. The media can tell that story and generate more in the pursuit of a policy that may solve the problem. Governments may cooperate with the humanitarian organization as instruments of policy and with the media as conveyors of its purpose. But it is an unequal triangle. Both the humanitarian organizations and the governments count on their aid and their policy to succeed. The media have their story either way—success or failure. Yet for all their cables and wires and lenses and modems, the media are people, too, and not without feelings. They don't set out to record failure, but take what comes.

Here is an opportunity to develop a modus operandi for these three in surveying and solving the humanitarian problems of the world. Governments, humanitarian organizations, and media are likely to be working in close quarters more often than ever before. Each can profit from better understanding the workings and motivations of the others.

The hungry, oppressed, and afflicted of the world could be better off for this book.

—Charles Bierbauer
Senior Washington Correspondent,
Cable News Network

Preface

As codirectors of the Humanitarianism and War Project, we are pleased to make available this study as a resource for the international community as it struggles with a daunting number of humanitarian tragedies and civil wars.

Launched in 1991, our project is an independent policy research initiative situated at the interface between theory and practice. The data for our work has been drawn from interviews with more than 2,000 practitioners both on the frontlines and in the relative security of headquarters. Their concerns and insights have informed an array of publications for a wide variety of readership, including guidebooks and training materials for humanitarian practitioners; monographs with recommendations for policymakers; journal articles for academics; and op-ed pieces and books for the concerned international public. This range of publications reflects our conviction, and that of the organizations providing us with resources, that policy research that does not change the ways in which humanitarian activities are conceived, mounted, and supported will have failed to achieve its full potential.

Three sets of institutions—the media, humanitarian organizations, and government policymakers—make up what may be called a *crisis triangle*. Their interaction is of increasing salience to the outcomes of effective humanitarian action. Gone are the days in which success was determined principally by humanitarian organizations themselves. The news media, it seems, have become a major humanitarian actor in their own right, helping to frame the context within which government policy is formulated and humanitarian action is mounted. While the growing role of the Western news media that constitute the main focus of this study is widely acknowledged, the dynamics of interaction with government policymakers and humanitarian practitioners have received little analytical scrutiny to date. The exploration of these dynamics in this volume represents one early step in a long and complex analytical journey.

The present study seeks to highlight the common ground shared by the three sets of institutions, broadening the current working perspective held by each of the other two. Detailing not only the interests but also the limitations on the involvement of each in the humanitarian sphere, the study aims to increase mutual understanding and cooperation. None of the three has an exclusively humanitarian agenda; none can function in ignorance of the others. Whereas aid agencies are the principal intended audience of this study, newcomers to the humanitarian arena from the media and from government also may find it useful. In addition, the analysis may challenge assumptions held by more seasoned professionals and stimulate reflection on the issues by the organizations and practitioners involved.

- For the government policymaker, this handbook seeks to supply insights into more-effective use of the media and humanitarian networks, helping to minimize some of the perennial frictions.
- For humanitarian agencies, it highlights the importance of nurturing professional relationships with the media, mindful at the same time that the media have multiple agendas and functions.
- For the media, it is designed to provide an analysis of humanitarian issues and organizations, encouraging wider and better reporting of crises and, equally important, focusing on the need to prevent rather than cure.

Although this volume stops short of a set of do's and don'ts for the major players, our traditional emphasis on the practical is present. We frame key issues and offer specific suggestions about how each set of institutions might function more effectively and accountably in the humanitarian sphere. We expect our presentation to provoke discussion in boardrooms, newsrooms, situation rooms, and classrooms. We are pleased that the International Centre for Humanitarian Reporting is exploring the possibility of adapting into booklet form for use by media professionals some of the practical experience reviewed here. Several consortia of NGOs are also considering similar adaptations for humanitarian practitioners.

We wish to acknowledge the contributions of a number of institutions and individuals to this publication. The published text reflects comments on an earlier draft made by a wide array of colleagues, too numerous to mention by name. Special thanks are due to those who participated in workshops in Geneva, Switzerland, and in Washington, D.C., in October 1995 and to the organizations that joined the Humanitarianism and War Project to cohost these working sessions. Cohosting the Geneva workshop were Peter Walker from the International Federation of Red Cross and Red Crescent Societies and Edward Girardet and Sue Pfiffner from the International Centre for Humanitarian Reporting. Cohosting the Washington meeting were Peter Shiras and George Devendorf from InterAction, and Robert Nevitt, Richard Melanson, and Colonel David Tretler of the National War College.

This volume also builds upon collaboration between the Humanitarianism and War Project and the World Peace Foundation. Papers prepared for a conference held in December 1994 appeared subsequently in a collection of essays entitled *From Massacres to Genocide: The Media, Humanitarian Crises, and Public Policy,* edited by Robert I. Rotberg and Thomas G. Weiss.

Arranging meetings to solicit comments and preparing this study for publication would not have been possible without energetic support from staff at the Watson Institute. We would like to acknowledge in particular the contributions of Fred Fullerton, Richard Gann, Amy Langlais, Suzanne Miller, and Jennifer Patrick. Colin Scott, a project consultant, has provided essential staff work, including initial research and interviews, framing of the issues, drafting the initial text, and assistance in the two workshops.

This publication has been made possible by a generous grant from the Pew Charitable Trusts of Philadelphia. We would like to express our gratitude to Nadya Shmavonian and Catherine Murphy for their confidence in and support of this undertaking. Publication of this volume has also been assisted by a contribution from the Disaster Management Training Program of the UN Department of Humanitarian Affairs. Resources have also been applied from other contributors to the Humanitarianism and War Project, almost forty to date, which are listed by name at the end of the book. Their support has been essential in making possible the ongoing research and other activities of the project.

There is much yet to be learned about the interactions reviewed here. In fact, as new civil wars erupt and as existing ones take new forms, some of the analysis and insights offered here will require review and updating; we encourage readers to annotate, amplify, and amend this text accordingly. As always, we welcome comments on the starting point provided here.

—*Larry Minear*
—*Thomas G. Weiss*

Introduction

CONVENTIONAL WISDOM AND CONFLICTING EVIDENCE

Humanitarian crises accompanying civil wars have been a feature of the first five years of the post–Cold War era. Large-scale human suffering has been both a cause and a symptom of fragmenting states. The passing of the Soviet-U.S. bipolar era has witnessed a new willingness, articulated by the United Nations Security Council, to identify internal armed conflicts— once largely outside the purview of international scrutiny—as threats to international peace and security and thus as the objects of concerted international action. The resulting task of mounting humanitarian action, however, has become more complicated, more dangerous, and more problematic than in yesteryear.

Headline-grabbing crises such as those in Somalia, Rwanda, the former Yugoslavia, and Haiti have revealed complex relationships among the *crisis triangle* of policymakers, humanitarian agencies, and the Western news media. This three-sided interplay has elicited considerable comment. The media are depicted often as a decisive causal link between a given crisis and the reaction of the international community, forcing the pace and sometimes the direction of government policy formation and humanitarian action. Yet little is known about how that interaction works and its implications for effective humanitarian action.

Evidence of what has come to be called the *CNN factor* remains highly anecdotal. Although neither humanitarian crises nor their reporting is new, the proliferation of both in an era of high-speed communications has led to widespread speculation about the influence the media may exercise. The news media are widely supposed to have increased pressures on government policymakers, both directly and through the information provided to the public. Some suspect that the need for officials to be seen doing "something" now outweighs the need to do "the right thing." Others counter that the media are not a serious factor in the formulation of policy; rather, they only influence its presentation. The underlying assumption that the media have the power to pervert or distort rational policy processes, while arguably true in some recent situations, has not been examined as a more general proposition.

Figure 1
The Crisis Triangle

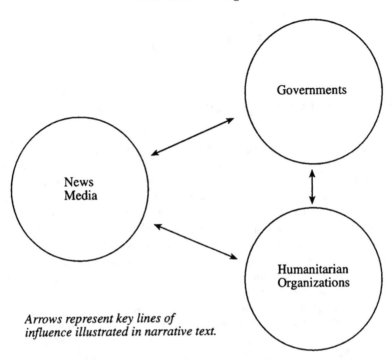

Arrows represent key lines of
influence illustrated in narrative text.

Similarly, the media are widely thought to influence the work of humanitarian organizations. Media success in putting crises into the living rooms of potential donors and in augmenting the resources that aid groups have at their disposal is widely acknowledged. But do the media also influence the dynamics of the crises to which humanitarian organizations flock, the jockeying for position that results, the kinds of activities mounted? How significant is the pressure of the press, what are its positive and negative consequences, and what strategies are needed among humanitarian organizations for coping with it? Decisions about how many resources to invest in media relations and how high a priority to give the training of staff in that area would benefit from a clearer understanding of the impact of the media.

Empirical research and scholarly analysis reviewing relationships between the news media and policymakers on the one hand and humanitarian organizations on the other have been surprisingly scant.[1] The dynamics of the interaction are little understood—indeed, whether the impact of the news media on humanitarian action is revolutionary, evolutionary, or largely imagined remains for the most part a matter of conjecture. The purpose of this study is to examine the crisis triangle, with a view to improving the quality of humanitarian action by strengthening the contributions of all three parties to more-effective policy, humanitarian action, and journalism.

Media images of human suffering have motivated people to express their concern and their solidarity with those in distant places by contributing to relief efforts and by demanding explanations and action from governments. The media's influence on the shaping of foreign policy is considerable in many countries.
— Commission on Global Governance[2]

Media roles in publicizing crises, influencing public opinion, and reporting international response are nothing new. Do the humanitarian emergencies in Biafra in the 1960s and in Bangladesh and Ethiopia in the 1970s and 1980s provide precedent for the current debate? In these crises, media coverage had an irresistible effect on mass audiences, producing surges of fund-raising and humanitarian responses.[3] What is the current reality of reporting and response? Do the media stimulate better policy and humanitarian action or just encourage short-term mobilization of resources? And how will these processes be changed by the proliferation of media channels and the speed with which any number of crises can now be spotlighted?

In the recent spate of post–Cold War crises—Somalia provides a good example—was the international response television-led? Did the media retard more-effective response by not reporting the crisis early enough and then stimulate a panic response late in the day? Why was the intervention in Somalia not preceded or followed by similar action in nearby southern Sudan, where humanitarian conditions had been worse for years? Was that neglect due to lack of TV coverage, or were other factors at work?

Relentless coverage of inhumanity in both Bosnia and Rwanda, matching the intensity of that directed toward Somalia in late 1992 and early 1993, failed in either case to produce Somali-style interventions. Although massive coverage of the situations in Sarajevo and Goma has been linked to a variety of international response, none of them appears to have constituted decisive or durable changes in policy. British Foreign Secretary Douglas Hurd asserted in September 1993 that policy was not and should not be dictated by the media.[4] Yet hurry-up measures by governments to help the Kurds in Iraq or evacuate certain Bosnian war victims given high media profiles seemed to reflect causation rather than coincidence. The nature and extent of the media's influence on policy generate more questions than answers.

Those questions, however, do require answers. Building on the growing awareness among many international actors of the media's potential for powerful humanitarian consequences, a more detailed assessment from the humanitarian community of the media is required. Are the media a unitary actor that manipulates events or a complex process or set of processes that are themselves subject to manipulation? Are there not differing effects on policy and humanitarian action of news, documentary, and other types of coverage, and differing impacts from television, radio, and print media? Given economic pressures facing media outlets to tell a good story more quickly and compellingly than their competitors, is the role of the media to inform or entertain?

The aim of this study is to improve the quality of humanitarian action (while understanding that objective is not necessarily the overriding consideration for policymakers and the media). All three sets of institutions have the potential to help improve the way the international humanitarian regime functions, and a self-interest in expanding the scope of cooperation. Identifying the potential and constraints of the media requires more than talk of the CNN factor and other glib generalizations. Challenging conventional wisdom and presenting conflicting evidence is the first stage in a more realistic assessment, and the overall objective of the following pages.

> *CNN is the sixteenth member of the Security Council.*
> —UN Secretary-General Boutros Boutros-Ghali 1995[5]

METHODOLOGY

This study continues the approach of utilizing the varied experience of practitioners to understand the dynamics and idiosyncrasies of humanitarian action and to suggest practical improvements (*see* Minear and Weiss, *Humanitarian Action in Times of War*). It is based upon discussions with seasoned professionals from each of the three sets of institutions. It reflects findings drawn from various country case studies conducted by the Humanitarianism and War Project between 1990 and 1995, augmented by interviews, conducted during 1994–1995, specially designed to identify the media's roles.

In reviewing the complex interactions within the crisis triangle, there are no magic formulas to be discovered and applied. However, as each new crisis draws a fresh contingent of policymakers, aid workers, and reporters, a wealth of experience from previous crises continues to remain untapped. Institutions have weak collective memories, and individuals move on to different responsibilities.

The lessons drawn from recent experience range across areas of political science, international relations, journalism, and development studies; analytical expertise across disciplinary lines is clearly needed for understanding the interaction. This volume relies on practical experience rather than any single discipline and on individual illustrations and provocative experiences rather than on quantitative evidence. A theoretical framework within which the often contradictory data may be organized remains desirable but elusive.

SCOPE

This book examines the role of external actors in a selected number of *complex emergencies:* that is, political crises within states that have involved armed conflict and widespread social upheaval. Humanitarian responses to such crises the take two basic forms of action: emergency and rehabilitation assistance for affected populations, and protection measures to prevent abuses of basic human rights. External initiatives originate with a wide range of intergovernmental, governmental, and nongovernmental bodies. International responses frequently build upon—but sometimes also can pre-empt—remedial action by institutions internal to the crisis areas themselves.

Emergency and Rehabilitation Aid

Emergency aid offers short-term humanitarian assistance, usually in the form of life-saving measures such as food, shelter, and medical care. Although various organizations differ in what they include within the term, emergency aid is distinguished from medium-term rehabilitation and longer-term developmental aid and usually is funded from separate budget sources. Functional and institutional links exist between emergency and nonemergency aid, making their separation for conceptual, programmatic, and budgetary purposes arbitrary and questionable.

Emergency aid in complex emergencies is generally provided within one of three broad types of security framework. First, it may be *consensual.* That is, the aid activities are accepted by the controlling political-military actors and given freedom of access to civilian populations within their jurisdictions. Second, emergency aid may be *protected.* In such cases, aid is usually negotiated through and delivered under the auspices of external military force. Third, aid may be part of a package of *coercive measures,* backed by military force or a threat of force. Whether a given framework is consensual, protected, or coercive will have a bearing on humanitarian strategies.

Looking beyond the meeting of immediate needs, humanitarian agencies view *rehabilitation* as a way out of a crisis. (Rehabilitation is also termed *recovery* or *reconstruction* by some.) An investment in the promotion of self-sufficiency among client populations and in the prevention of recurrent conflict, rehabilitation activities often start with some form of demobilization or demilitarization. A longer-term goal is to rebuild governmental and private infrastructure, a task that has become urgent in many countries because the systematic looting of physical assets and the elimination of trained human resources have been specific war aims.

The progression in assistance from emergency through rehabilitation to long-term development is now described as the *aid continuum*. Though experience has taught us to question the idea of a linear or sequential approach, donor policies and statutory and budgetary definitions perpetuate a division of aid categories, often with little tolerance for the "gray areas" confronted by aid agencies on the ground. In the Commission of the European Union, for example, responsibility for emergencies and for reconstruction and development activities are in two different directorates altogether.

The growing discontinuity between emergency aid and other efforts has become a major policy concern. In recent years, attention has been directed to providing emergency aid in ways that establish momentum for medium- and longer-term efforts. Conversely, the provision of emergency aid may affect negatively the prospects for rehabilitation and longer-term self-reliance of recipients whose coping capacities have been undercut by relief activities.

In its broadest sense, humanitarian action includes longer-term development assistance as well as emergency and rehabilitation aid. The fact that rehabilitation and development are invariably less well-funded and less energetically pursued than relief is also mounting cause for concern. Critics of the imbalance often fault the media, moving quickly as it does from one crisis to the next, for failing to give adequate attention to the post-emergency challenge.[6]

Human Rights Protection

A related concern, often institutionally separated from the provision of emergency, rehabilitation, and development assistance, is the prevention of human rights abuses. As well as working to ensure physical protection of vulnerable populations, humanitarian and human rights agencies monitor and publicize abuses, lobby governments, and nurture a broader constituency in support of their efforts. Publicity, especially in the form of media coverage, is often crucial to accomplishing their objectives. In addition to the need for monitoring in their own right, human rights violations also may provide an early warning of social or political upheaval and thus of the eventual need for emergency assistance.

Human rights protection and various forms of assistance are integral parts of humanitarian action broadly conceived, but exercising the protection function may present a dilemma for agencies whose primary purpose is assistance. Such groups face difficult choices when witnessing human rights abuses that place aid operations in jeopardy. Human rights agencies traditionally have been separate and distinct from relief organizations, with relatively little interaction between their respective staff, programs, and constituencies. Recent complex emergencies, in which human rights abuses have been used as weapons of war, have increased the degree of contact. Targeting the safety and security of minority groups, like interdicting their food supplies, are related threats to humanity that challenge all humanitarian actors.[7]

The spread of television and reporting by satellite have made it possible to provide audiences in industrial countries with graphic images of large-scale human misery. This has raised the awareness of western audiences to disaster situations and increased public donations to relief efforts. At the same time it has influenced the approach to disasters, sometimes promoting expensive gestures which relieve the sufferings of a few individuals but divert attention from the difficult political and technical work needed to relieve the situation as a whole.
—1994 DAC Chairman's Report[8]

ORGANIZATION

Chapter 1 sketches the external institutional landscape, situating the three major actors—government policymakers, humanitarian organizations, and the media—that respond to complex emergencies. Each side of the crisis triangle is described with reference to its agendas and interests, its range of responses to humanitarian crises, and its limitations. (Since the chapter is designed as something of a primer, readers familiar with these institutions may wish to proceed to the following chapter, or limit their reading to the actors with which they are least familiar.)

Chapter 2 assesses the three-sided interaction among external actors in several complex emergencies and offers some preliminary findings. Recent experiences in Liberia, Northern Iraq, Somalia, the former Yugoslavia, Haiti, and Rwanda are noted in detail, and some provisional findings that emerge from those experiences are identified.

Chapter 3 articulates recommendations for each of the sets of institutions appropriate to the political and economic contexts in which they are likely to be operating. The objective is better media coverage, better policy, and better humanitarian action. Means of increasing the accountability of each of the actors also are suggested.

The book concludes with a glossary, a list of acronyms, a bibliography, information about the authors and the participants in the workshops at which an earlier version of this study was reviewed, and about the Humanitarianism and War Project and the sponsoring institutions.

Chapter One

External Institutions in Civil Wars

Any attempt to capture the vigor, complexity, and idiosyncrasies of inter-action among government policymaking institutions, humanitarian orga-nizations, and the media will suffer from oversimplification. None of the three institutions in the crisis triangle is monolithic. In humanitarian crises they do not operate in isolation from one another, but interact in many ways. They function in a particular geopolitical moment in which Western states, under the critical eyes of the media, attempt to evolve foreign poli-cies out of ad hoc reactions to post–Cold War changes.

Interactions among the three are complex. Governments not only make policy but also have their own implementing humanitarian agencies. Many governmental and private humanitarian organizations seek to influ-ence the processes and results of public policy formation. All implement-ing agencies are subject to decisions reached by policymakers and may be subject to media scrutiny. All those with an interest in humanitarian crises, whether governmental, intergovernmental, or private, share analytical and operational problems. In carrying out their functions, individuals from all three groups seek contact and cooperation with the others, regardless of their own institutional affiliations.

The distinct perspectives of the three sets of institutions provide a log-ical starting point for analysis. Governmental institutions are concerned primarily with decisionmaking; humanitarian institutions are charged with implementation; and the news media are concerned with reporting on crises and responses. This chapter considers the interests, structures, and limitations of each set of institutions; Chapter 2 reviews their interactions.

GOVERNMENTAL POLICYMAKING INSTITUTIONS

What Are the Interests and Responses of States?

The tendency of states to avoid involvement in the internal conflicts of other states, an axiom of international relations for centuries, has been tested in recent decades by growing interdependence. With the passing of the Cold War era, conflicts within states and their accompanying humanitarian consequences have become a preoccupation of governments and the United Nations system. "[A]ll of us feel our humanity threatened," U.S. President Bill Clinton has observed, "as much by fights going on within the borders of nations as by the dangers of fighting across national borders."[9] Why do states respond, or fail to respond, to humanitarian crises? What is the range of response at their disposal?

Governments respond to humanitarian crises for a variety of reasons, but one senior government policymaker has noted three major kinds of pressure. First, the *humanitarian imperative* reflects an obligation perceived by governments to respond in instances of widespread suffering (though humanitarian reflexes rarely operate in isolation from other forces and factors). Second, *domestic political agendas,* which carry a multitude of players and power-brokering, also come into play. Third, the exercise of *international responsibilities,* whether in the form of providing emergency assistance or peacekeeping troops, has come to be regarded as a necessary element in global leadership.

Send charitable aid under the Red Cross to both sides, and for the rest—keep out of it and arm.
—Winston Churchill, on the Spanish Civil War, 1937[10]

Beyond altruism, there has been in recent years a greater readiness to define humanitarian crises as a *threat to international peace and security* requiring a collective response in the spirit of the UN Charter. The expansion of the traditional definition of such threats follows a recognition of their potential to spread chaos and conflict to neighboring states, strengthening their claim on some kind of collective action. In practice, the international community has responded with a range of measures, including various forms of outside military force (though experience in Liberia, Bosnia, Rwanda, and Somalia has demonstrated the limitations of ill-conceived military action, even when mounted to support humanitarian operations).

Whether or not they provide peacekeeping or other troops, states often are ready to support emergency and rehabilitation aid. Such assistance may be offered as a palliative, as a political alternative, or as a potential peace-builder. High-profile humanitarian action often becomes a substitute for, rather than a complement to, political-military strategies. The need for peace and security measures along with humanitarian action is apparent, but their joint application often is not well-defined or well-executed. Frequently, even if the provision of humanitarian aid depends upon favorable political and security conditions, the cost of military action—especially when accompanied by casualties—may be judged too high. Moreover, the use of force to secure aid may jeopardize the neutrality of humanitarian operations in the eyes of belligerent forces.

These dilemmas are most apparent in the UN system, where governmental policymakers have made considerable rhetorical—and some tangible—investment in joint political and humanitarian efforts. The UN Secretary-General rarely has received the necessary backing from the Security Council to adopt such a comprehensive approach. Field operations are not like the UN Charter, there is no clear dividing line between security and humanitarian roles. The two functions come together under joint management in the command structure of the United Nations; increasingly, both are vested in in-country Special Representatives of the UN Secretary-General (SRSG). Yet effective joint management of the two spheres of operation often proves elusive.

The spirit of robust humanitarianism that was characterized by international actions in Iraq and Somalia has ebbed. Humanitarian agencies cannot depend on the guarantee of security from outside military forces within which they might safely operate. (In fact, some keep their distance from such forces as a matter of policy.) Instead, they have been left with the prime responsibility of working aid into the cracks of crumbling political regimes, or worse, into the anarchic ruins of disintegrating states. Rhetoric notwithstanding, there has been a demonstrated lack of international resolve to improve coordination of the panoply of governmental, intergovernmental, and nongovernmental aid efforts. In 1992, General Assembly Resolution 46/182 sought better coordinated aid through a new UN Department of Humanitarian Affairs, but without the resources or institutional power to fulfill such a mandate. As a government policymaker said, "coordination is the last thing governments want, it means giving up sovereignty."

How Do Policymakers Respond?

The making of public policy involves a range of institutional processes in numerous stages, all subject to political bloodletting and other factors extraneous to the specific humanitarian challenge. Although the processes rarely involve a precise progression, the following enumeration of stages provides a useful framework for identifying and analyzing the impact of the media and government responses to humanitarian crises. Alternative and nonlinear models may be equally helpful in reaching useful conclusions about how certain crises find a place on the government's agenda.[11]

Agenda Setting: Problem Identification

The model suggests that there is a priority list of issues to which government officials and their outside interlocutors are paying attention at any given time. Of course, agendas vary among levels of government. Even apparently minor humanitarian crises will have the attention of some specialized official at one level or another. However, being "on the agenda" is taken to mean the serious attention of senior policymakers reflecting the concerns of ministers of state, heads of aid agencies, legislators, or senior military staff.

Delineation of Alternatives: Solution Formation

Once a crisis has been placed on the agenda, a set of alternatives for government action is formulated for consideration by senior officials and their close associates. In major crises, governments can consider a range of alternatives (military, diplomatic, and/or humanitarian measures) through unilateral, regional, and multilateral means and using private and/or governmental channels. Most governments have both routine and expedited structures for devising options and responding to crises.

Selection of Alternatives: Policy Adoption

This stage involves "an authoritative choice among . . . specified alternatives, as in a legislative vote or a presidential decision."[12] In the United States, the commitment of troops, at least initially, is an executive branch function, although the fact that the Congress holds the purse strings makes consultation advisable. In Europe, the wide dispersion of powers at the national and international levels makes it difficult to generalize about action in humanitarian crises. Individual European governments, although free to act unilaterally through their own structures, have options (and feel increasing pressures) to give preference to Europe-wide institutions for policy, emergency aid, and military responses.

Implementation of Decisions

Once problems have been identified, alternatives framed, and courses of action chosen, the focus of attention turns to the agents of action. These include ministries of defense and/or NATO for military intervention, foreign ministries and their aid departments for political and aid responses. Here, too, distortion of policy implementation may result from media attention or even extended public relations by governments. This stage might involve "mission creep," as policy goals that were originally narrowly framed expand as a result of physical exigencies on the ground.

Predecision processes remain relatively uncharted territory. We know more about how issues are disposed of than we know about how they came to be issues on the governmental agenda in the first place.
—John W. Kingdon[13]

The complexity of the international system that responds to humanitarian crises hinders tracing policy processes through these different stages. In both bilateral and multilateral settings, states may respond at the political-security and humanitarian levels. In practice, there are myriad institutions and processes, all with policymakers pursuing their own ideas and agendas and responding to varying kinds of pressures. Coordination of policies across and within states often is hard to detect, if in fact it exists at all.

What Are the Limitations on Governmental Responses?

The media and humanitarian organizations may criticize governments for not responding effectively to complex emergencies wherever they exist, but there are in fact major limitations on the action by governments. Three are examined here: political constraints that complicate the effort to frame the proper context for humanitarian action; organizational inflexibilities that make it difficult for government bureaucracies to respond; and finally, resource limitations that dramatize the need to rank humanitarian crises in order of relative priority. These various constraints will be examined in greater detail in the six case studies in Chapter 2.

Political Limitations

Although perceived national interests and political and electoral concerns usually explain the actions of states, they may also represent a major limitation on humanitarian action. Three governmental approaches to managing the tensions between humanitarian action and political considerations are evident.[14]

The first subordinates humanitarian action to politics. This approach was most apparent during the Cold War era when U.S. aid was weighted toward countries under communist threat while Soviet aid went to those pursuing communist agendas. In the post–Cold War era, aid carries economic and political messages, such as the promotion of free-market economies or multiparty democracies. Aid is also linked to the purchase of donor country services or products. Although emergency humanitarian aid is ostensibly more free of such conditionalities, its political value is being increasingly recognized, representing yet another limitation on the independence of humanitarian action.

The second approach uses humanitarian aid as a palliative, in effect a substitute for dealing with the root causes of crises or for taking more robust action. A single government or a group of governments that cannot agree on a more decisive action may find in humanitarian assistance a lowest common denominator. The results are often unconvincing or counterproductive.[15] In some cases aid may even prolong the conflict by inadvertently supplying warring factions and easing the pressure for more decisive diplomatic or military action. Recent expenditure trends, which favor emergencies at the expense of development, have fueled a concern that donor governments are not really serious about dealing with the root causes of humanitarian crises.[16]

The third approach balances political and humanitarian operations, retaining a certain independence for aid activities. Striking a proper balance means neither conditioning emergency aid on the existence of a prior political settlement nor tying a political settlement to the provision of such aid. In El Salvador, the peacekeeping efforts of ONUSAL and the humanitarian activities of the UN and other aid organizations manifested a productive synergism. The U.S. approach to Haiti after September 1994, replacing the earlier, unproductive sanctions-only policy with military backing for humanitarian goals, resulted in benefits to both the political and the humanitarian side.

Whereas the choice of approaches varies according to the donor government and the emergency, certain trends are emerging. The European Union's Humanitarian Office (ECHO) risks subordinating humanitarian activities to the perceived need for greater visibility in aid efforts. Given the difficulties experienced in forging a common European foreign policy, humanitarian activities, on which greater agreement has been possible, have been given heightened prominence.

Meanwhile in the United States, humanitarian assistance, although no longer an instrument in Cold War politics, has not been liberated completely from political agendas. Andrew Natsios, who headed the Office of Foreign Disaster Assistance during the Reagan administration, has observed that "U.S. foreign disaster assistance has been drawn into an increasingly intimate connection with American foreign policy by the geometric increase in complex humanitarian emergencies, by the growing use of food as a weapon of war and the diplomatic interventions needed to guarantee access to it, by the increasingly intense State Department focus . . . and by the institutional weakness of the United Nations in responding."[17] The continuing close connection between humanitarian assistance and foreign policy runs the risk of subordinating saving lives and reducing suffering to extraneous political objectives.

Organizational Limitations

Finding the proper political context within which to situate humanitarian action is only one of the constraints under which donor governments labor. A second category of difficulties concerns organizational or bureaucratic limitations. Humanitarian action by governments, mediated through a complex multilayered set of institutions, is often affected by bureaucratic interests. The institutional apparatus through which governments respond to complex emergencies involves a bewildering array of sometimes

*P*otential political/diplomatic benefits from humanitarian aid:

• *A preventive measure to stave off chaos in an unraveling society*

• *A confidence-building measure during political negotiations*

• *A means to protect democratic and economic reforms*

• *A way to implement peace accords . . .*

• *An effort to mitigate the effects of economic sanctions on the poor, where sanctions serve geopolitical ends*

• *A means to encourage a political settlement by contending factions*

—Andrew Natsios, vice president of World Vision International and former head of the U.S. Office of Foreign Disaster Assistance[18]

conflicting executive, administrative, military, and legislative elements. In the United States, responses are coordinated by the executive branch, but a variety of pressures emerge from the policy processes in the White House (including the National Security Council), the State Department, the Pentagon, and the Congress. Operational responses to crises continue to come from the State Department's Bureau for Refugee and Migration Affairs and from AID's Bureau for Humanitarian Response, which includes the Office for Foreign Disaster Assistance. With greater political attention paid to these crises, nontraditional elements, such as the Defense Department's Office of Human Rights and Refugee Affairs, have increased their involvement in policy and operations.

European governments exhibit a similar array of institutional actors, with decisionmaking processes equally complex and perhaps a bit less transparent. Even the Scandinavian nations, which separate aid departments from foreign ministries to mitigate the risk of political interference, have multiple offices involved. In Western Europe, the institutional architecture is complicated further by an extra layer of response through the European Union (EU). An EU member government may respond to a crisis bilaterally through its aid ministry, and, since 1992, with a multilateral option through ECHO. Governments may insist on their own visibility, whether channeling resources through national or European vehicles. Even in working multilaterally, they may insist on preference for the utilization of NGOs or suppliers from their own nation.

Decisionmaking and coordination, difficult within individual governments and within groupings of governments such as the EU, become even more problematic when the arena is broadened to include the United Nations system, where organizational rivalries, political-aid tensions, and budgetary and turf concerns are legendary. The bureaucratic confusion that results at every level creates problems for humanitarian organizations that receive funds from governments and provides the media with an easy target.

Resource Limitations

Governments face the claims of a seemingly unlimited number of crises with decidedly limited resources. They cannot avoid picking and choosing among the emergencies to which they will respond. To guide decision-making, they attempt to establish priorities among crises. Criteria used include such indicators as the nature, scale, and severity of the suffering, the proximity or accessibility of its location, the nature of the assistance needed, the comparative advantage that a given government may have in providing such assistance, and the donor government's historical relations with the affected country, government, and people.

What makes one humanitarian crisis more important than another? U.S. President Bill Clinton has offered the following comment on the prioritization process: "This era has seen an epidemic of humanitarian catastrophes, many caused by ethnic conflicts or the collapse of governments. Some, such as Bosnia, clearly affect our interests. Others, such as Rwanda, less directly affect our own security interests, but still warrant our concern and our assistance.[19]

Defining a nation's interests, and then applying such determinations to the crises that exist at a given time is a difficult process. Some argue, for example, that social and environmental chaos springing from internal conflicts is the new enemy, the containment of which should be the center-piece of Western foreign policy. If so, the classic test of national interest will need radical revision to guide responses in most civil wars of the post–Cold War era.[20]

From a humanitarian standpoint, the dangers of ranking crises are legion. If all life is precious, how would an intervention in a crisis be justified at 100,000 deaths but not at 10,000? At the same time, without some specific criteria, how do policymakers avoid conveying the impression that Bosnian lives are more important than Sudanese, Rwandese, or East Timorese lives? The Geneva Conventions specify that authentic humanitarian assistance is to be based exclusively on need, devoid of extraneous agendas. However, various criteria used by governments to apportion scarce resources have political elements, as does the bureaucratic process through which allocations decisions are vetted.

Whatever the intellectual construct used to establish priorities, the criteria are often tested by new crises in unanticipated ways. Presidential Decision Directive 25 (PDD 25) of May 1994, which defined U.S. national interests narrowly and laid down multiple preconditions for committing U.S. troops overseas, reflected Washington's wrenching experience in Somalia. However, PDD 25 proved unsatisfactory when confronting its first major test: genocide in Rwanda. PDD 25 was invoked in the months after the beginning of the genocide in April 1994 to forestall action urged by other countries to reinforce the UN peacekeeping force there, a stance for which the U.S. was roundly criticized. Later in the year, when the administration itself sought to expand UN presence in Rwanda, PDD 25 created obstacles to doing so.

In summary, government policymaking is inhibited by political constraints, organizational inflexibilities, and resource limitations. Each prevents the evolution of consistent policy and impedes the abilities of governments to respond effectively to humanitarian crises. Humanitarian action reflects the multiple and sometimes internally inconsistent agendas of governments. In the tensions between domestic and international priorities, humanitarian agendas generally come last and are rarely, if ever, overriding. Operative definitions of national interest and prioritizations of emergencies currently provide little space for independent humanitarian action. Budgetary constraints and inflexibilities among various kinds of assistance discourage longer-term preventive and reconstruction measures. Complex emergencies thus expose a gap in governmental competence that the media may highlight and help remedy.

> **V**ital national interests *pertain when "the survival of the U.S. or key allies, critical U.S. economic interests or the danger of a nuclear threat" all require a readiness to risk military action, as with Iraq and North Korea.*
>
> Important, but not vital, national interests *pertain in cases such as Bosnia and Haiti, where "some level of force" should be considered, but used "selectively" and "commensurate with U.S. interests.'*
>
> Humanitarian concerns *pertain where U.S. military forces should only be used if their "unique resources" can counter humanitarian "catastrophes," such as Rwanda, which "dwarfs the ability of normal relief agencies to respond." The risks to U.S. personnel should be "minimal."*
> —Secretary of Defense William J. Perry, on U.S. interests and the use of force[21]

HUMANITARIAN INSTITUTIONS

What Are the Interests and Responses of Humanitarian Institutions?

Humanitarian institutions require review and analysis according to the same categories as government decisionmakers: that is, their interests, responses, and limitations. Humanitarian organizations also are characterized by their diversity, a quality that often confounds interlocutors in governments and the media alike. Like governments, humanitarian agencies are themselves in transition from the period of East-West tension, which made significant inroads on the integrity of their activities, to the post–Cold War period, a time of new challenges requiring responses that are still being devised.

Although humanitarian institutions include a wide range of governmental and nongovernmental organizations, embrace diverse philosophies, and rely on a variety of constituencies of support, they all espouse the humanitarian imperative: the alleviation of life-threatening suffering.

Like the International Committee of the Red Cross (ICRC), founded in 1864, many humanitarian groups, such as UNICEF, Save the Children, and Oxfam, have their origins in nonpartisan relief programs for victims of war. While firmly committed to the preventive value of long-term development, emergency aid has remained a highly publicized part of their

Figure 2
The Humanitarian Network[22]

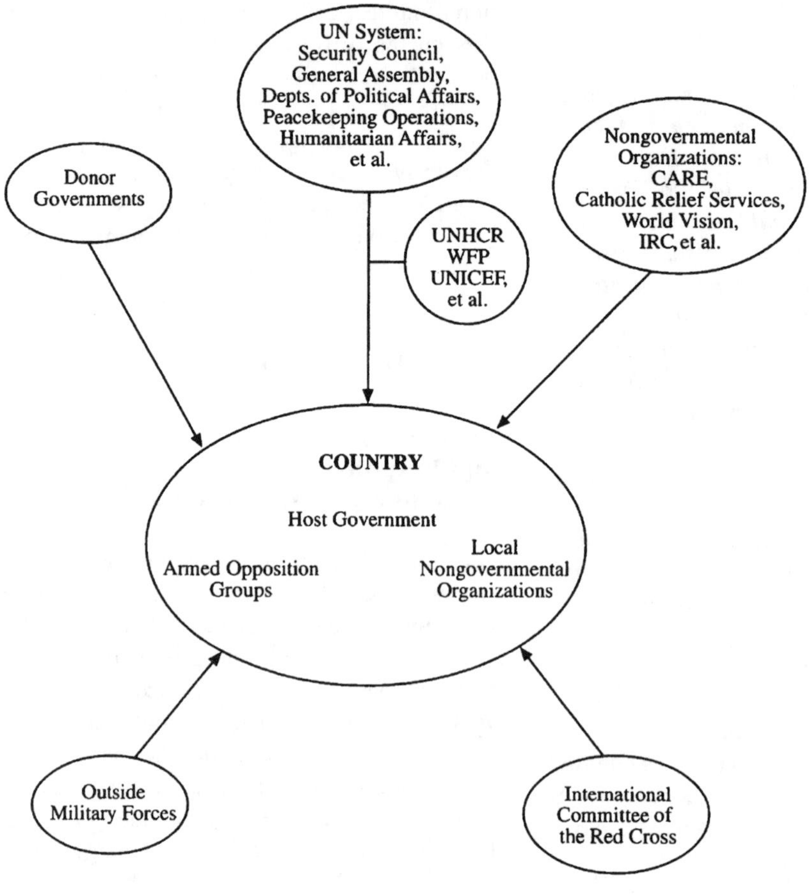

work. However, the proliferation of complex emergencies since 1990 and the heightened expectations of international responses have put a special burden of responsibility on established agencies as well as creating a host of newcomers. Each of the five broad categories of agencies requires review: UN organizations, donor government agencies, NGOs, the ICRC, and the military.

The United Nations System

The task of responding to humanitarian need is lodged with individual organizations, principally the United Nations Children's Fund (UNICEF), the UN World Food Programme (WFP), the United Nations High Commissioner for Refugees (UNHCR), the United Nations Development Programme (UNDP) and the World Health Organization (WHO). United Nations Volunteers (UNV) provide personnel to assist in complex emergencies. Although most of these agencies have as a primary objective the promotion of long-term development, they all also have mandates to respond to emergencies, with emergencies units to manage their activities.

Each of the organizations has its own mandate and its own governing body made up of representatives of governments. UNICEF focuses on the needs of women and children, UNHCR on refugees, and WFP on food assistance. Such mandates obviously overlap. The resulting problems of coordination have led to periodic calls for a single consolidated UN organization to handle emergencies. While conceptually attractive and potentially cost-effective, such an entity could widen existing disconnects between emergency assistance and rehabilitation and development aid. A single UN relief agency also could worsen the existing imbalance in funding to the further detriment of nonemergency programs.

A second circle of UN organizations has significant but more peripheral involvement in emergency response activities. These include the UN Food and Agriculture Organization (FAO), the UN Educational, Scientific and Cultural Organization (UNESCO), and several activities administered by UNDP, including the UN Fund for Population Activities (UNFPA), the UN Development Fund for Women, and the UN Capital Development Fund (UNCDF). Also a part of the UN system are regional organizations such as the Economic Commission for Asia and the Pacific (ESCAP), which are generally not involved in program operation.

A third circle is made up of the Bretton Woods institutions: the World Bank and the International Monetary Fund. Formally a part of the United Nations system, these organizations have independent charters and governance and stress their separateness from the UN. Although the World Bank's resources are not normally committed to emergencies, they are increasingly available for rehabilitation as well as development purposes.

IMF policies and loans have a direct bearing on the economic and political prospects for governments beset by and recovering from civil wars. Similarly involved are the regional lending institutions in the World Bank family, such as the African and Asian Development Banks.

In a category by themselves are other intergovernmental organizations which are not formally part of the UN system. These include regional entities, such as the Organization of African Unity (OAU) and subregional groups such as the Economic Community of West African States (ECOWAS), which may play diplomatic or peacekeeping roles. There are also intergovernmental organizations, such as the Geneva-based International Organization for Migration (IOM), which has a more limited membership of governments and a focused mandate on assistance to refugees and the internally displaced.

Since 1992, a coordinated UN response in complex emergencies has been the responsibility of the Department of Humanitarian Affairs (DHA) in the UN secretariat. Created in the wake of disjointed UN programs in the Gulf crisis, DHA has enjoyed neither the financial nor the administrative leverage for its demanding task. DHA provides support for the Inter-Agency Standing Committee (IASC), a forum that draws together on a quarterly basis representatives of the major UN organizations, NGOs, and the ICRC for information-sharing and coordination purposes.[23]

As a result of such efforts, coordination has been strengthened within the UN system, although there remains considerable room for improvement. DHA spearheads efforts to do joint assessments of individual humanitarian crises, to make joint appeals on behalf of the entire system, and to track the contributions that result. Its reports have become the source of the most comprehensive data on responses by the international community to major humanitarian emergencies, although not all funds contributed are listed in the reports. DHA is also engaged in efforts to evaluate the performance of the UN system in emergencies, although the most rigorous evaluations are made by evaluations units of individual UN organizations.

DHA also provides the focal point for coordination with the other two major UN departments engaged in complex emergencies: the UN Departments of Peace-keeping Operations (DPKO) and Political Affairs (DPA). The interface among these three departments (among which DHA is the weakest) is where humanitarian and political-military activities are addressed. The three under-secretaries-general heading each department report to the Secretary-General, who takes direction from the Security Council.

At the country level, the UN official charged with coordination of the humanitarian response is the UNDP resident representative in his or her capacity as resident coordinator of the UN system. In major emergencies, a separate humanitarian coordinator may be appointed by DHA. In some crises, particularly before DHA's creation, one of the operational UN organizations was appointed "lead agency," with certain coordinating responsibilities for the UN family of agencies. In circumstances in which the Secretary-General appoints a special representative (SRSG) to head an operation, the humanitarian coordinator may report to that person as well as to DHA in New York.

Separate from the UN family of assistance organizations and outside the coordinating ambit of DHA and the IASC is the UN Centre for Human Rights. Contrasting in its modest size with the more programmatic and operational UN organizations, the Geneva-based center is an arm of the UN Human Rights Commission, a body made up of fifty-three UN-member governments that meets in two regular sessions each year. Until the recent spate of emergencies, the commission has had few international staff resident in countries in crisis, instead dispatching special rapporteurs to report on human rights abuses.

Donor Governments

Donor governments are the source of most of the resources available for humanitarian action, whether channeled to UN organizations and NGOs or used by governments to operate their own substantial assistance programs.

At the opening of the Second Development Decade in 1970, governments in the UN General Assembly adopted a target of 0.7 percent of their gross national products (GNP) as the level of their commitment to official development assistance (ODA). The target was framed not only to encourage financial contributions but to allow comparability among donors based on the relative size of their economies rather than on the absolute size of their aid budgets. As indicated in Figure 3, only the countries of Denmark, Norway, Sweden, and the Netherlands reached that target in 1993. The preeminent donors—the United States and Japan—fall far short of the target at 0.15 and 0.26 percent respectively.

U.S. resources frequently amount to between one-third and one-half of total bilateral government commitments to humanitarian crises. Washington remains the preeminent donor to emergencies, often setting the pace and the trend of responses. However, its leadership position has eroded in recent years, in part reflecting a falling off of resource commitments and in part a broader U.S. retrenchment in multilateral cooperation. The member states of the European Union, individually and jointly through ECHO and the European Union's Development Directorate, represent, along with Japan, the other major blocs of resources.

Well aware that the decisionmaking and prioritization processes vary from one country to the next, governments seek to coordinate and harmonize aid policies through the Development Assistance Committee (DAC) of the Paris-based Organization for Economic Co-operation and Development

Figure 3
ODA by Member Governments of the DAC, 1993[24]

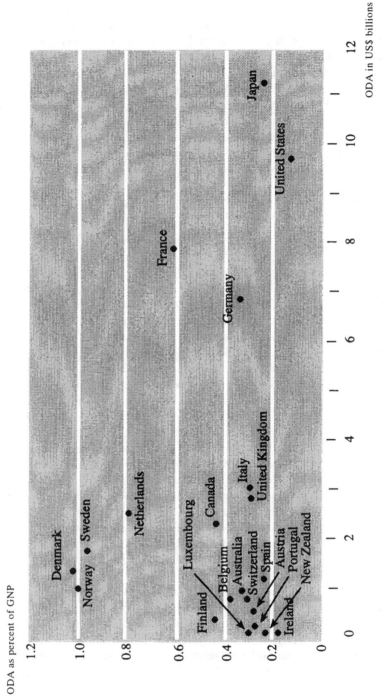

Source: James H. Michel, *Development Co-operation: Efforts of the Members of the Development Assistance Committee* (Paris: OECD, 1995), 77.

(OECD). The annual DAC Chairman's Report provides a useful review of international perspectives on the issues discussed in this chapter.[25] Yet the DAC has had difficulty in addressing qualitative as distinct from quantitative aspects of emergency and other official development assistance. It has not established consensus on the relationships between emergency, rehabilitation, and development assistance or on whether the contributions of national military forces should be credited as ODA.

DAC figures are instructive in highlighting the growing share of official development assistance directed toward emergencies (see Figure 3). "Emergency assistance and distress relief, which had constituted less than 3 percent of bilateral aid until 1990, had come to exceed 8 percent of the total by 1993," the DAC chairman reported in 1994. "Expressed in current dollars, what had been a $300 million item in the early 1980s had become a $3.2 billion claim on bilateral aid budgets in 1993."[26] In 1994, humanitarian assistance to Rwanda alone totaled an estimated 2 percent of all ODA.[27]

In recent years, DAC chairmen have expressed concern about a leveling-off and falling of aid levels. The 1994 report showed a drop in aid levels from $60.8 billion in 1992 to $56.0 billion in 1993. This represented an 8 percent reduction in current dollars (6 percent in real terms), with the aid contributions of 17 of 21 DAC member countries failing to hold their own. Taking a hopeful view, the DAC report interpreted this troubling development as "a bout of weakness, rather than an incipient collapse" in the fabric of aid cooperation.[28] A recent NGO review was more negative. "In spite of growing prosperity in DAC donor countries, and the consistent support of the OECD public for efforts to help the poor," the analysis concluded, "the era of gradually growing assistance for the poor seems to have come to an end."[29]

The extent to which "donor fatigue" is a new fact of international life is a matter of debate. The loss of interest among the publics in donor countries is frequently cited by governments as a major factor contributing to a falling off of aid levels. The alleged loss of interest is contested by NGOs, who, pointing to public opinion polls that show continued strong support for programs of development cooperation, charge that governments are using "donor fatigue" as a rationalization for their own lackluster performance. The media often use the term, unaware of the debate surrounding it.

Nongovernmental Organizations

The third category of humanitarian agency comprises nongovernmental organizations. The multitude of international NGOs ranges from large-scale international federations that respond to most major crises to individual agencies with programs in selected continents or emergencies. More than 1,000 NGOs have been granted consultative status by the UN's Economic and Social Council (ECOSOC), and for every organization accredited there are scores that are not. Many developing countries and nations in crisis have their own NGOs, some of which are linked to international networks while others are not. Individual UN organizations and donor governments have their own rosters of international and national NGOs, which overlap with, but differ from, those accredited to the United Nations.

There is no internationally recognized working definition of a nongovernmental organization, nor are the distinctions clear between NGOs and other categories of private sector institutions, such as grassroots organizations and solidarity groups. NGOs are a loosely defined group of institutions whose purposes are often public but whose resources are privately generated and managed. Many have charitable or nonprofit status in their countries of origin, entitling them to receive individual donations on a tax-deductible basis, but imposing certain constraints regarding such matters as advocacy and accountability. Many are linked to religious networks; many are rooted in secular constituencies.[30] Some, such as Médecins Sans Frontières (MSF), concern themselves with emergencies only; others, such as Oxfam, address both emergencies and development.

Although many NGOs are modest in the scale of their activities, a few, such as CARE and World Vision, have access to more resources for work in a given country than UN organizations, donor governments, or even government ministries themselves. NGOs were so numerous and so active in Haiti in 1994–1995 that Haitian government officials referred disparagingly to their country as a "Republic of NGOs." Mozambican officials called their country "the Donor's Republic of Mozambique."

Donor governments often regard NGOs as advantageous partners in emergencies because their energetic and low-cost operations help victims at the grassroots, a population that governmental and intergovernmental programs often fail to reach. Quick responses, direct action in danger zones, and a willingness to operate where other actors face political constraints make them an attractive conduit for both public and private funds.

NGOs include agencies concerned with human rights protection as well as those providing emergency relief. Again, NGOs have comparative advantages vis-à-vis UN organizations and governments that also seek to address such issues. Groups such as Amnesty International and Human Rights Watch have greater freedom and willingness to speak out against abuses than governments or the UN human rights machinery. Often exposure of individual abuses or an evolving pattern of abuse signals a broader erosion of internal security and a threat of wider humanitarian problems.

In recent years, NGOs have paid greater attention to effectiveness and accountability. This trend has been spurred by factors such as the greater prominence NGO work has attained in headline crises, the higher degree of complexity involved in functioning effectively in civil war settings, and the increased scrutiny that their activities have received from governments and the media. Professional associations of NGOs, such as the Geneva-based International Council of Voluntary Agencies (ICVA) and the Washington-based coalition of U.S. agencies, InterAction, have been an arena for reviewing current standards of professionalism. The International Federation of Red Cross and Red Crescent Societies (IFRC) has taken the lead in developing and promoting a voluntary Code of Conduct among NGOs.

International Committee of the Red Cross

In a category of its own, the ICRC is a neutral body established in international law to assist and protect individuals in both international and non-international armed conflicts. Custodian of the Geneva Conventions of 1949 and the Additional Protocols of 1977, the ICRC enjoys a special status in international law and an observer role in the UN General Assembly. Donor governments traditionally fund about 90 percent of its $500 million annual budget. The base of the organization in Geneva, Switzerland, underscores its commitment to neutrality. Traditionally, most ICRC international staff have been Swiss nationals, but the ICRC in recent years has utilized professionals from other countries in responding to emergencies. Specialized personnel, such as doctors or logisticians, may be non-Swiss, although the heads of the ICRC's delegations remain Swiss.

The ICRC has been the most visible private organization in interstate and intrastate armed conflicts. Its staff are generally in the vanguard of international personnel working in areas of potential conflict. In conflict after conflict, it emerges as the single most sought-after and trusted source of information by the media. A member of the Inter-Agency Standing Committee and sharing information on emergencies with the United Nations, the ICRC is nonetheless careful to maintain its distance from UN peacekeeping and political activities. Best known among humanitarian organizations that practice the "consensual approach," it requires agreement of all belligerents in a given conflict before it will provide assistance to civilians in any one area. Its mandated responsibilities include visits to prisoners of war and political detainees as well as assistance to civilian populations.

The best-known among Red Cross institutions, the ICRC is in fact only one of three component parts of the Red Cross and Red Crescent movement. The other two are the (180) national Red Cross and Red Crescent Societies and the International Federation of Red Cross and Red Crescent societies (IFRC). The division of labor within the movement is such that whereas the ICRC has responsibility for the victims of international and internal armed conflicts, the IFRC is tasked with responding to natural disasters and the needs of civilian populations in nonconflict settings. Individual national societies have their own mandates, which include assisting in emergencies within their own borders, managing blood donation and volunteer programs, and mobilizing financial and personnel resources for international deployment.

All members of the Red Cross movement, which meet together in an International Red Cross Conference at multiyear intervals, subscribe to seven principles: of humanity, impartiality, neutrality, independence, voluntary service, unity, and universality. In practice, these principles compete with one another and are often difficult to implement. The ICRC works to ensure that the contributions it receives for particular crises are not "earmarked" in ways that undermine the organization's independence and impartiality. National societies often find the requisite independence difficult inasmuch as government officials normally serve on their boards.

The Military

A fifth institution, in some respects an element within the UN and donor government categories, comprises external military forces. This relative newcomer to the humanitarian arena has contributed significantly to recent efforts by traditional humanitarian organizations to respond to emergencies. During the Cold War the military forces of various nations were sometimes mobilized to combat the consequences of natural disasters, but their contribution to the delivery of relief and protection of human rights in war zones was limited to occasional actions of unilateral forces or of national contingents serving in UN peacekeeping operations.

However, beginning with the creation of safe havens for Kurds escaping Iraqi aggression, in April 1991, outside military forces have been increasingly pressed into service in complex emergencies. Sometimes, troops have operated under national authority, as in the case of U.S. troops in Somalia. Sometimes they have served in coalitions of forces, as in northern Iraq or Haiti. More frequently, they have served under multilateral authority in UN peacekeeping operations, as in Somalia, the former Yugoslavia, Cambodia, and Angola.

International military forces have performed three basic roles in the humanitarian sphere. They have fostered a climate of security for civilian populations and humanitarian organizations; they have provided direct support to the work of such organizations; and they have engaged in direct assistance and protection activities themselves. Whereas the contribution of the military in a number of recent crises has been indispensable, the extent to which it will become a permanent feature of the international humanitarian system is unclear. At issue are several unresolved policy questions, such as cost and cost-effectiveness, comparative advantage, cultural differences with humanitarian organizations, and the often negative consequences of utilizing military forces.[31]

In addition to these five sets of international humanitarian actors, there are also institutions within the countries in crisis that often play a major humanitarian role. These include the political authorities—governmental or insurgent; the military forces of the warring parties; and the institutions of civil society. These national actors do not figure prominently in this book because the focus is on international organizations. The roles of national actors, however, should not be minimized or ignored.[32]

What Are the Limitations on Humanitarian Responses?

Mandates, Funding, and Ties to Donors

Every humanitarian organization operates under certain constraints. Each is limited to one degree or another by such factors as its constitution and mandate, constituency and traditions, geographical area and client group, operational sector and expertise. No single organization assists every person in every country with emergency, rehabilitation, or development assistance. Available resources are generally provided for specific purposes in stated settings for stated periods. As a result, partnerships are often sought with governmental, intergovernmental, or nongovernmental agencies, which further complicates funding and coordination.

In recent years, the proliferation of emergencies and of agencies seeking to provide assistance has increased the demand and competition for funds. As indicated earlier, a greater proportion of overall aid budgets are now being directed toward emergencies. UN organizations and donor governments are making greater use of NGOs as subcontractors. For NGOs that rely on such resources, limitations on the location and type of aid operations inevitably follow. If donors themselves lean in the direction of televised crises, the effect is carried over to NGOs whose funding depends on government allocations.[33] Even NGOs that rely for most or all of their resources on private contributions are affected by the media-mediated priorities of individual contributors.

Tensions Between Emergency and Longer-Term Approaches

The relationship between emergency and longer-term assistance remains a conceptual and operational hurdle for many humanitarian agencies. As already described, many organizations respond to emergencies but see themselves primarily as agents of long-term development. This means, on the positive side, that they approach emergencies with an eye to addressing the underlying causes of humanitarian crises. On the negative side, it contributes to an institutional schizophrenia among groups that would rather not be involved in emergencies at all. Agencies that see themselves as providing essentially a short-term, life-saving service often become involved necessarily in prolonged emergencies and issues of rehabilitation and reconstruction. Despite the fact that some donors are more flexible in their approach, funding criteria reflecting a continuum from emergency relief through rehabilitation to development greatly complicate program planning and operations.

Security

There is widespread agreement that a basic level of security is essential for all humanitarian operations. A problem less pronounced during the Cold War, humanitarian organizations have achieved little community-wide consensus on how best to achieve it. Working in highly volatile conflicts, humanitarian agencies are faced with the difficult choice of negotiating their own safety and access from a position of humanitarian independence or integrating their operations within a political-security framework. The military can offer unparalleled security and logistical advantages that may be valuable for a time, but humanitarian workers tend to be more willing to take risks than are the military assigned to protect them. Moreover, their association with armed forces may compromise their neutrality in the eyes of warring factions or of civilian populations. Military forces deployed to protect assistance for one group of victims may be perceived as the enemy by others.

Several alternative approaches have been taken by aid organizations to the challenges posed by multifactional violence in settings such as Liberia, the Sudan, and Somalia. Some have sought to negotiate the passage of assistance through the battle lines. Negotiating agreements is consistent with the principle of impartiality and in keeping with the voluntary nature of assistance but is often rejected by warring factions. Others have relied on the use of superior military force to shield relief operations. The use of military force, while often more effective in the short term, risks compromise by association with a political-military strategy and is difficult to sustain. A third option involves temporary suspension or permanent cessation of aid operations, an apparent admission of defeat for those with humanitarian mandates.

The ICRC adopts the first approach. UN organizations, situated within the United Nations system, often take the second approach, although they sometimes express reservations about being too closely associated with the UN's political-military strategies and timetable. NGOs, which have more freedom to choose the path of independence or to associate themselves with a given security framework, have yet to agree in various conflicts or, as a general matter of principle, on one approach or the other.

Coordination and Competition

Better coordination at the international level and within individual crises is always in demand. Indeed, there is a chronic lack of coordination at both levels. However, there is little agreement about what coordination involves and considerable reluctance by individual organizations to submit to it.[34]

Competition among humanitarian agencies is a distinguishing feature of virtually every emergency. Fund-raising and publicity are the lifeblood of aid agencies, whether they are seeking governmental or individual support. As a result, jockeying for the attention of the media and donors is routine. The agency competition that characterized aspects of the Rwanda emergency in May 1994, especially the infighting for the attention of the media, appeared to overwhelm established coordination systems.[35] As the numbers and types of agencies multiply, the lack of regulation is likely to stimulate further competition for turf and a part of the fund-raising action. The centrifugal pressures of competition counteract the centripetal forces toward cooperation.

Several interagency mechanisms already have been mentioned that play a role in different aspects of coordination at different levels. These include the UN Department of Humanitarian Affairs, the Inter-Agency Standing Committee, the Development Assistance Committee of the OECD, and professional organizations of NGOs, such as Geneva-based International Council of Voluntary Agencies and Washington-based Inter-Action. Additional coordinating vehicles are a European Union–NGO forum and a Disasters Emergency Committee in the United Kingdom. In individual crises, ad hoc coordinating mechanisms—either among NGOs or encompassing NGOs and other humanitarian actors—are also established.

The United Nations would appear to provide the logical vehicle for coordinating in-country operations. However, as noted earlier, some organizations have reasons of principle and policy for refusing to allow themselves to be coordinated. As a result, coordination arrangements in a given crisis are generally ad hoc, hammered out on the ground at meetings of practitioners. The chemistry among the organizations and individuals involved as well as the nature of the crises mean that results are difficult to predict.[36]

With an increasing number of players, more complex political terrain, and heightened expectations by the international public, the guiding humanitarian principle is often obscured in the crowded landscape of internal armed conflicts. Moreover, as the number of agencies has increased, values beyond altruism have emerged as powerful forces. Disaster relief is now big business, with agencies competing for their own market share.

Their needs for funding pressure agencies into demonstrating results to both public and governments—the latter an increasingly critical source of finance.

NGOs are generally acknowledged to be more cost-effective and represent the major operational partner for much assistance from the UN and donor governments. However, the subcontracting of such aid to private groups does not necessarily guarantee greater efficiency or cost-effectiveness. The ten largest U.S. and European NGOs now control about 75 percent of emergency delivery. Agencies with multi-million-dollar budgets are every bit as powerful—and, some would argue, as bureaucratic—as are similar-sized organizations. It is evident that humanitarian organizations struggle with forces that may threaten their humanitarian agendas and dilute their effectiveness.

Prioritization

As with governments that are forced to establish priorities in allocating finite resources among multiple conflicts, humanitarian agencies face tortuous choices about where to deploy resources and personnel. They, too, are faced with shrinking resources. Moreover, the aid budgets of major donors since 1990 have shifted to perceived priorities in areas such as the former Soviet Union and Eastern Europe. "The policy 'commitment' which many donors have given [that] aid to the [Central and Eastern European countries and newly independent states] will not be at the expense of developing countries is difficult to monitor," concludes one recent independent review. "But it is nevertheless the case that funds have been found for aid to the East at a time when aid to the South is being cut."[37]

Even within Africa, certain "loud emergencies" such as Somalia and Rwanda have attracted more international attention and funds than the relatively silent emergencies such as Sudan and Liberia, to say nothing of the really silent emergencies in Sierra Leone and Burundi. Some agencies have followed available money while others have attempted to sustain interest in the forgotten crises and unpopular sectors. NGOs are likely to have more difficulty in resisting donor government trends in this area; even in the life-and-death task of setting priorities, the relationship between pipers and tunes does not change.

THE NEWS MEDIA

What Are the Interests of the Media?

Studies of the media abound, but there is little agreement on a satisfactory definition or serviceable understanding of the term. Many people involved in preliminary discussions for this book, including a number of journalists, were dissatisfied with the term, although they provided no satisfactory alternative. The following description is not intended to recast academic theory on the media but to distill and reflect the experience of a variety of experts whose profession involves interacting with the media in one capacity or another.

The media are no less complex an institution than government policymaking or humanitarian organizations. The moving parts are equally numerous, the processes equally resistant to reduction to linear models. Yet the media are often dismissed as a monolithic actor, single-mindedly bent on exploiting humanitarian crises as sellable news at the lowest possible newsgathering cost.

Policymakers and humanitarian agencies frequently complain about what they consider disproportionate media influence over elected officials and public opinion. The same critics are often equally dismayed, however, if the media stay away from crises altogether. The media are criticized often for the superficial knowledge of international affairs that prevails among major segments of the U.S. population. In reality, the prevailing illiteracy implicates public institutions, policymakers, and even humanitarian organizations.[38] It is clear that the media have become a favorite scapegoat, the more so as new technology has appeared to augment their influence.

Rather than approaching the media as an actor with a purpose, it is more instructive to view the media as an institution with a process. In fact, using *media* in the plural may help to disaggregate their multiple agendas and interests in humanitarian crises. A more disaggregated approach offers a closer analysis of the differential effects of various forms of journalism on various audiences, including policymakers and the general public.

It is also helpful to review more closely the commodity of the system, news information, which originates in many forms and is subject to many influences. Before reaching the media, information is handled by a host of stakeholders, many of whom are influenced not by the objective news value of a given event but by political, professional, or commercial motives. Within media institutions such information is moved forward, changed, or discarded via an editorial funnel managed by a series of "gatekeepers." In addition to gatekeepers who measure the comparative value of news information, other professional and idiosyncratic forces—only some of them journalistic—are at work determining what will be produced and conveyed.[39]

Despite these multiple interests and influences, the product that emerges from the system bears much uniformity across competing sections of the media. As a foreign news radio editor said, "No one in the media wants to take the chance of being wrong, so they stick to consumers' views of the news." At the same time, while commercial competition may contribute to a certain uniformity in news coverage, different media inject

Good news is too often considered not newsworthy. Bad news is not "news" until it offers good visual images. Murder in a small town and its big-time equivalent, war within or between nations, makes better news than a nutrition program that improves a million lives.
—Carole Zimmerman[40]

different commercial criteria and, in some cases, political considerations that affect the content and style of coverage. Since the product is available to policy elites and public alike, the media is regarded by some observers as a lowest common denominator within which multiple actors in a crisis find themselves reduced to a common field of arbitration.

Humanitarian Priorities Within the Media

The news media in general and journalists in particular are wary of suggestions that they have, or should adopt, a humanitarian agenda. As in other sectors where special interests seek expanded coverage of activities in which they are involved, the proposition that the media give special attention to humanitarian issues is viewed as a flagrant violation of journalistic ethics and a step down a steep and slippery slope. There are several respects, however, in which the humanitarian interests of the media directly affect the ways in which a given news institution functions. Those interests are evident first in the establishment of priorities among news subjects and angles and, second, in the humanitarian instincts and personal objectives of working journalists.

The varying approaches of the media to humanitarian issues are illustrated by an exchange between two journalists at one of the workshops convened to discuss this volume. A reporter from a weekly news magazine described the media as "morally neutral." "The media doesn't have a humanitarian mission," she observed. "We simply report what we see." News about humanitarian matters competes quite properly for attention with business, sports, entertainment, and other news.

An editor from a daily paper agreed that a "humanitarian correctness" test that injected a positive spin into events or an arbitrary balance between good news and bad would be a mistake. At the same time, she applauded the fact that her newspaper described its approach as "humanitarian" and "international" in its selection of reporters and in the marching orders it gives them, in its use of the editorial page, and in promotional materials sent to potential subscribers. Within the media as an institution, she concluded, "There is a place for a presumption of concern for all humanity."

The workshops also led various journalists to articulate why they chose the news media as a profession, what they hope to accomplish, and what are the sources of their greatest professional satisfaction. Some journalists carry a strong personal humanitarian agenda, take great personal risks in reporting conflicts and suffering, and are committed to seeing that their work contributes to a more-effective global response. One participant, speaking in personal terms of why he worked for years as a journalist and is now an editorial writer, spoke with passion of his interest in the world and its people. "I want to be involved with news that does solve problems, that does make a difference."

The involvement of reporters in war zones also has produced numerous examples of actions outside the call of journalistic duty. One reporter recounted personally shepherding a youngster across a closed bridge from Rwanda into Zaire, negotiating with the authorities in order to reunite him with his parents. In conflict after conflict, journalists strike up not only working relationships but also friendships with humanitarian personnel. While they must work to preserve their objectivity as reporters, the fact that they take more than a professional interest in the issues is undeniable. Their reporting helps establish, and builds on, a palpable human interest among news consumers.

How Do the Media Respond?

Among the many professional and accidental factors involved in determining media coverage, three are key in analyzing media response: the net news value of a particular crisis, the type of news coverage, and the structure of the news industry. New technology, in particular the use of satellites to bring real-time television coverage of far-away events, already has brought some profound changes to the nature of media responses.

What Makes the News?

News information, the commodity of the media system, may appear to be the result of arbitrary selection from a mass of materials assembled in random and chaotic fashion. However, a glance at daily headlines and bulletins in competing markets demonstrates a striking consistency in output. Attempts to determine whether that consistency reflects an intrinsic objectivity in news coverage or, more negatively, the uniform currency created by the demands of competition have confronted analysts with a maze of contradictory data.

In his classic study, *Deciding What's News,* Herbert J. Gans provides a useful checklist for "story importance." He assesses news according to its rank in governmental and other hierarchies, impact on national interest, numbers of people affected, and significance for past or future developments.[41] Stories meeting one of the criteria grow in importance if and when they satisfy the others. However, the outcome is more often a matter of journalistic judgment than of absolute values. Editors also apply other "product tests" in the selection process, notably the novelty of the story and its suitability for the particular media format.

Defining news as merely "what the editors say it is," however, may overlook a process that filters information long before an editor reaches a final decision. Moreover, editors with one eye on the relative news values of their reporters' offerings may have another eye on the commercial and political priorities of their publishers and proprietors. Understanding news as the dynamic commodity within such a process qualifies any notion of an intrinsic or net news value. Competition is crucial. "Note the impact of a few national news organizations" on the decisions that other media make, said one editor who considers the *New York Times*, the *Washington Post*, the networks, and CNN to be "the relatively few trend-setters."

What Types of News Coverage Operate?

News information comes to the consumer at different speeds in various packages with different shelf lives. For the purposes of this analysis, three broad categories of news coverage are identified. Television and radio news bulletins as well as news sections of print media constitute what might be called headline news. The emphasis is on reporting the latest developments in fast-moving or breaking stories and scooping the opposition rather than on presenting an in-depth analysis of events.

Documentary news, which enjoys a longer shelf life, may offer more detailed background and unpacking of an issue, demonstrating the investigative or analytical skills of a particular news outlet or reporter. This kind of coverage is typically found in specialist broadcast features and on inside pages of newspapers and journals. Some newspapers have little space for documentary news and, in their allocation of what they have, give preference to local or national over international topics.

A third category, news commentary, is represented by editorials or opinion pieces that carry a particular point of view on the issues of the moment. Such commentaries are an extension of policy processes, often used by governments and policy elites to make their own views known. Use by nongovernmental commentators also demonstrates the autonomy of news organizations and represents an obvious source of media impact on policy. News commentary provides perhaps the most obvious vehicle through which publishers and editors can communicate their institutional or personal viewpoints.

These three broad categories of news information are not mutually exclusive, but overlap and interact among themselves. Although the distinctions seem obvious, all three affect differently the formation of public policy and the shape of humanitarian action. Policymakers and aid groups often overlook how much modern news information is tailored to different audiences, with different style and content.

How Are the News Media Structured to Respond?

Within the news industry, a broad division exists between electronic and print media. Each has maintained a separate niche in the commercial and news market while using the other as a source. Television and radio journalists regularly scan newspapers and journals for story ideas; the print media often utilize their greater capacity to follow up headline news items in more depth. Many journalists—and some policymakers as well—admit to using CNN as a kind of wire service for monitoring fast-breaking stories. Changing technology, in particular the development of electronic newspapers and interactive television, may blur the remaining distinctions between electronic and print media and rearrange the gatekeepers in the system.

Much of the post–Cold War debate about media influence on foreign policy has focused on television as the most potent actor.[42] Drawing upon satellite technology, television news bulletins depict the violence and suffering of conflicts with an immediacy and realism that, some argue, forces a rapid policy response. If the so-called CNN effect exists—and the review of recent humanitarian emergencies in Chapter 2 contains traces of it—that effect necessarily would be limited by television's selectivity in covering crises. Moreover, the production expense of television, especially with respect to foreign news, is such that sustained coverage often depends on radio or print media to uncover a story in the first place and to maintain its public profile once the cameras have left. The value of television news dramatizing events needs to be balanced against the selectivity and episodic nature of its coverage.

The media also need to be differentiated according to their basic market audience or readership. Although they have access to a global pool of pictures and to far-flung (albeit largely English-speaking) reporting, the majority of media are still national in focus. So, too, is the content of most news programs and publications. Even services such as CNN or ITN World News that are marketed as global invariably reflect U.S. and British domestic perspectives and values. Commercial demands also have blurred the traditional division of news media into those serving "quality" as distinct from "tabloid" markets. Electronic and print media are now finely tuned in content and style to link audiences or readership with advertisers. Increasingly, the media have to resort to packaging news in a new form of tabloidism that mixes information with entertainment. Judging from the reception, the resulting blend dubbed "infotainment" is both profitable from a commercial standpoint and questionable from a journalistic one.

Several international media organizations stand out as noteworthy exceptions to these trends. These include the BBC World Service radio and the *International Herald-Tribune* newspaper, which maintain high standards of comprehensive reporting and are regarded as sources of authenticity in international affairs. This is not to say that such media are necessarily influential in the highest levels of policy processes. As a British government policymaker noted, only a limited number of broadcast institutions such as BBC Radio News and ITN bulletins exercise serious influence on senior officials and politicians. At the same time, there appears to be no necessary connection between audience size and policy impact. Several U.S. policymakers report watching CNN, whose domestic audience is relatively small.

Limitations of Media Coverage
in Relation to Humanitarian Crises

Analysts of how the media function in the area of complex emergencies note limitations in the sufficiency and adequacy of coverage provided.[43] Determining sufficiency requires a quantitative judgment, adequacy a qualitative one.

First, the amount of news coverage of complex emergencies is widely held to be insufficient. The number of major crises in which there is widespread and serious human deprivation and abuse of human rights outruns the coverage provided (unless, of course, a "major crisis" is by definition an emergency that receives international news coverage). At precisely the time when major crises have proliferated, many news organizations have reduced the space devoted to these events. That situation seems unlikely to change as commercial pressures continue to force a reduction in foreign newsgathering operations. "Most broadcast networks have severely cut back overseas operations," noted a foreign affairs correspondent, "often relying on footage drawn from other sources [which is then added] to a story written in London or New York."

In addition to being insufficient, current reporting of international crises also is widely held to be inadequate. Several areas have been identified in which the quality of news coverage has received specific criticism. One is that the media have provided too much attention to breaking events and too little historical and political context. A notable example to be examined in the following chapter concerns reportage of the Rwanda crisis. During the initial phase, when a preplanned campaign of genocide took place, international coverage was insufficient, with only a handful of reporters on the scene. Later, however, when hundreds of reporters chronicled the distress of Rwandan refugees in neighboring countries, coverage

*Y*ou know, when I first started in journalism I used to think that foreign correspondents spoke every language under the sun and spent their lives studying international conditions. Brother, look at us. On Monday afternoon I was in East Sheen breaking the news to a widow of her husband's death leap with a champion girl cyclist. Next day the chief has me in and says, "Corker, you're off to Ishmaelia." "Out of town job?" I asked. "East Africa," he said, just like that, "pack your traps." "What's the story?" I asked. "Well," he said, "a lot of niggers are having a war. I don't see anything in it myself, but the other agencies are sending feature men, so we've got to do something."
—*Scoop,* by Evelyn Waugh[45]

was inadequate. Few journalists noted that the population in refugee camps was composed of Rwandan communities transported largely intact, including political and military elements implicated in the genocide.

A second area of qualitative criticism is that the international media have focused on subjects of perceived interest to readers and viewers in developed countries. These include the threats posed by a given crisis to Western values, for example, and the activities of expatriate—generally North American and European—aid workers and the doings of Western troops. "It's a world through a Western prism," remarked a CNN reporter of much of the current coverage of international events. Among the results are a denigration of local institutions and an overemphasis on the relative importance of international and Western-led initiatives.

A third and related criticism concerns the perceived tendency of the media to perpetuate negative images and ethnocentric views. Persons affected by international crises often are portrayed as helpless victims who are dependent on, and take liberties with, international largesse. The fact that those who suffer are often nonwhite and their "rescuers" white has contributed to charges of racism in news coverage. Critics also speak of the "pornography of suffering," that is, of the dehumanization in their portrayal of those who suffer. On occasion, the beneficiaries of assistance have criticized the media and humanitarian institutions for the images conveyed.[44]

When Does an Overseas Crisis Make the News?

How does news about a foreign conflict or crisis penetrate the media as an institution? There are limitations both in the quantity and the style of coverage afforded to Western publics. International news stories still appear in even the most competitive category of headline news, although they are often compressed into a "roundup" or "newsbrief" format. Conflicts and disasters normally carry a high rating in decisions about what makes the news. That is especially the case if graphic pictures or first-hand reports are available and even more so if a particular country's aid personnel or soldiers are on the front lines.

However, difficulties of gaining access and the high costs of producing usable footage or reports can be prohibitive. Complex situations in war zones are frequently reduced to infotainment rather than treated in news documentary or news commentary format. Often a human interest angle is identified to emphasize the connection to a domestic audience. Sensing the difficulties in reporting the complexity of the conflicts in Bosnia and Rwanda, where "there are no good guys and bad guys, just bad guys and worse guys," Western journalists focused instead on efforts to arrange the medical evacuation of a single child from Sarajevo or to provide potable water for an individual family in Goma.[46]

Experience confirms that the domestic impact of an overseas story, actual or potential, is a key determinant of headline news. This is a variation of an old maxim that "bad news is big news," particularly in instances in which "bad news" is equated with a serious threat to national interests. As Herbert Gans explained the phenomenon, "[U.S.] journalists often follow American foreign policy in selecting foreign news because it supplies a quick and easy importance consideration and because no other equally efficient model is available." He also noted that "Foreign conflicts must be more dramatic and usually more violent in order to break into the news."[47]

International crises devoid of domestic interest rarely receive continuous or sustained coverage. The presence of international military forces invariably ensures coverage and provides the focus for the media of the troop-sending nation. U.S. military involvement in Somalia, Haiti, Rwanda, and Bosnia resulted in coverage far in excess of equally grievous humanitarian crises in Liberia and Sudan. Similarly, reporting on the activities of Canadian peacekeepers over the last several decades has provided the Canadian public with a major point of entry into international affairs. Dutch media were preoccupied throughout 1995 with the fate of Dutch peacekeepers in Srebrenica and a subsequent parliamentary inquiry about ethnic cleansing as the Serbs overran this so-called safe area.

Documentary news and news commentary, although using a broader trawl of issues, often take their lead from headline news. Nevertheless, while they, too, commonly emphasize tangible connections between "foreign" news and domestic interests, they may offer a wider point of entry for topics unwelcome or uneconomical in headline news. An interesting example of provocative documentary journalism was a 1994 article in *Atlantic Monthly* by Robert Kaplan, entitled "The Coming Anarchy," which portrays events in normally unnewsworthy West Africa as a harbinger of global chaos, the newest and latest challenge to U.S. foreign policy. Critics point out, however, that the piece also confirms many of the limitations of the news media. It was based on little academic research and on super-ficial understanding of the local context. In projecting U.S. perceptions and interests onto events that were in reality less chaotic than they ap-peared, Kaplan jumped to inappropriately apocalyptic conclusions.[48]

In summary, foreign news is often given highly subjective treatment by media committed to serving domestic markets. Moreover, the amount of coverage may decrease as the media reduce the amount of hard news. As a result, foreign conflicts carrying no obvious or immediate threat may be presented in the Western media only when they are advanced well be-yond the stage of prevention or containment. Even active conflicts are not assured coverage.

What Features of a Humanitarian Crisis Constitute News?

In 1995, an estimated thirty civil wars claimed at least a thousand deaths annually each, with all the actual or potential humanitarian costs accom-panying such strife. Judging from the resulting coverage, the media shared the difficulties experienced by government policymakers and humanitarian organizations in determining the allocation of limited resources among competing events. There appear to be no agreed-upon criteria by which the various news media determine the comparative newsworthiness of a given crisis. Various theoretical constructs have been offered about what *should* constitute news, yet the characteristics of what actually *does* constitute news are more elusive.

Danziger—© *The Christian Science Monitor*

Available data suggest that each crisis competes for coverage, not only with other foreign news stories but also with one another. As a general rule, the importance of a story may be related to the degree of perceived domestic threat. Thus, coverage in the United States of events in Iraq and Kuwait upstaged those in Liberia. In the Gulf War, "All the necessary themes to mobilize public opinion were in ample supply: freedom, dictatorship, self-determination, democracy and Western oil interests," noted one observer. "At the same time, Liberians were being massacred by rampaging tribal thugs. Yet . . . Liberia's plight was largely ignored."[49] The crisis in Liberia also was upstaged by Haiti; traditional ties to the West African country founded by freed U.S. slaves were overshadowed by the perceived threat of large numbers of Haitian boat-people.

With surprising regularity, the crises reviewed in Chapter 2 demonstrate that the attention given to one emergency came at the expense of another. As a result, the serious issue arises of whether the institutions of the crisis triangle—government policymaking and humanitarian action no less than the media—are able to keep the relative severity of multiple crises in view and respond accordingly.

In any event, the choices faced by the media in determining which crises to cover are complex, and multiple factors beyond perceived domestic threats often play a role in decisions. A major development, a fresh news angle, or an accumulation of events is often needed to attract the media to a conflict or crisis that otherwise would remain largely unnoticed. As recounted in Chapter 2, there was little coverage of the disintegration of the Somali state and the attendant civilian distress throughout most of 1991–1992. It was not until the latter half of 1992, when aid activities were increased—some of them designed to attract coverage—that the media accelerated reporting.

With respect to Rwanda, after months of limited coverage of genocide that claimed between 500,000 and one million lives, the following refugee emergency, complete with the specter of cholera, became the top international news story of the day. CNN, which was alerted to the likelihood of the outbreak of genocide in early April, opted against reporting on developments until three months later, when the genocide produced a mass migration of Hutus into neighboring countries. Contributing factors propelling increased coverage included the greater security and accessibility to the news media of Goma than Kigali and the involvement in the relief effort of many national military contingents and myriad humanitarian organizations.

Despite the lack of threat to Western strategic interests, both Somalia and Rwanda were stories with many newsworthy elements: civil war, extreme ethnic violence, refugees, and controversy about the nature of Western responses. Rwanda, suffering massive genocide, represented an

*T*he Advent and Domination of Real-Time Television:
• *Real-time images are those television pictures beamed back live by satellite from a location. Alternatively they may have been taped a few minutes earlier, or perhaps an hour or two beforehand—but little more.*
• *The presence of a satellite dish has created a new grammar and editorial agenda for TV news coverage.*
• *The absence of a satellite dish usually means significantly less TV coverage of a crisis. Often no dish means no coverage.*
• *The presence of a dish creates news coverage because of a TV news manager's corporate obligation to justify its costly deployment.*
• *In a war zone [real-time coverage] reduces the time span of the news cycle to a point where there is virtually no time lag.*
—Nik Gowing, diplomatic editor, Channel Four News, ITN[50]

affront to global human rights values and exposed the inability of the new world order to respond. The debate over intervention, linked to the definitional issue of genocide in international human rights conventions, raised Rwanda's profile in U.S. domestic and international politics. In general, however, humanitarian crises stand out only as signposts to newsgatherers of potentially newsworthy stories, subject to all the limitations already noted. It takes exceptional violence or some other distinguishing feature to lift them onto the screen or page.

How early in an emerging crisis does news coverage occur? This is a key issue for humanitarian agencies seeking to stimulate preventive action in a world in which government intelligence and policy systems fail to move incipient crises onto more visible agendas. The crises reviewed in Chapter 2 suggest a serious limitation in the attention of the media in the early phases. As did government policymakers and humanitarian institutions, the news media missed clear early warning signs in Somalia of the deteriorating situation and obvious forerunners in Burundi for what was to follow in Rwanda. The limitations of headline news in these various cases might suggest documentary coverage as a more likely agent of early warning. The overriding conclusion is more negative: the media should not be regarded as a substitute for other sources of intelligence for government decisionmaking apparatuses and humanitarian organizations.

SUMMARY

Figure 4 encapsulates the foregoing analysis of the three sets of institutions of the crisis triangle in operation, suggesting a surprising number of similarities among them. Each of the institutions is remarkably diverse, and none is a unitary actor. Each has institutional interests that affect its responses to humanitarian crises; each has limitations that impede its ability to respond fully. Each faces common challenges such as the need to set priorities governing its allocation of limited resources among the many conflicts that merit attention. None benefits from giving the impression of arbitrariness in its approach to emergencies. Each needs reliable information on which to base decisions, although for reasons of insecurity and lack of access is limited in its knowledge.

It is also apparent that, for all of their similarities, the three sets of institutions are fundamentally different. Governments serve national interests, humanitarian organizations serve the victims of conflict, and news media serve customers. None—including humanitarian organizations—has objectives that are exclusively humanitarian. Each has different points of accountability and standards of professionalism. The likelihood of friction and conflict, especially in dealing with situations that are themselves highly conflictual if not outright dangerous, is built into interactions.

Change is one factor faced by each institution in its respective field and function. Governments face a policy vacuum created by the new realities of the post–Cold War era. The media face a commercial and technological revolution with unfathomed positive and negative potential. The humanitarian agencies face increased entanglement with political and military forces and growing competitiveness across an ever-more crowded field.

These similarities, differences, and challenges emerge with greater specificity and concreteness from a review in Chapter 2 of recent crises. Drawing on that analysis, Chapter 3 highlights areas in which the three sets of institutions, individually and in their interactions, might improve the functioning of the international humanitarian system.

Figure 4
The Crisis Triangle in Operation

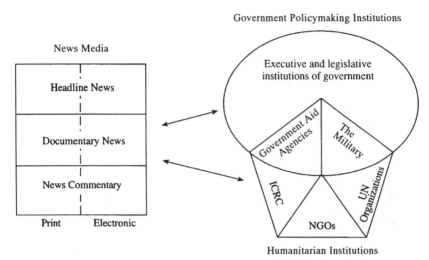

Arrows represent key lines of influence.
Note the degree of overlap betweeen governmental
and humanitarian institutions.

Chapter Two

Early Post–Cold War Experience

This chapter examines, in six post–Cold War crises, the relationship among the media, government policymakers, and humanitarian organizations. This examination illustrates some of the ways that the media do—and do not—influence policy processes and humanitarian responses.

Understanding the three-sided interaction requires assessing a daunting array of variables. No single model can do justice to the multifarious interplay among the institutions that make up the crisis triangle or capture the manifest and covert motivations of multiple actors operating across shifting political contexts. Without any scientific formula to explain or predict the outcomes of policymaking, this chapter examines the media-policy axis, assessing the contribution of humanitarian aid agencies to that set of relationships.

The effect of media activity on policy is itself intrinsically hard to measure. One stream of academic research has proceeded largely by interviewing policymakers who are eager or reluctant, as the case may be, to acknowledge the influence of the media. These individual experiences constitute raw data from which conclusions may be drawn, but it is often hard to decipher a large picture from separate anecdotes. Other analysts have taken a more "scientific" approach and have sought to draw conclusions about media influence based on quantitative calculations of media coverage in terms of column inches or broadcast time. Although this approach quantifies media coverage, it offers little insight into the impacts on policy.

Assessing causation—"influence" would be a more realistic word—is equally difficult when it comes to understanding the interactions between the media and humanitarian organizations. The crises reviewed in this chapter demonstrate an undeniable mutuality of influence: The news media influence the pace, scale, locus, and duration of action mounted by humanitarian actors. Conversely, those actors alert the media to breaking stories, provide them with first-hand accounts of what is taking place, and even arrange access for journalists to otherwise unreachable destinations and overnight food and accommodations in war zones. Yet calibrating the relative influence of the two institutions upon each other is almost impossible.

We can discern two divergent models of foreign policymaking. The traditional view holds that policymaking is the prerogative of an informed elite, with the media in derivative status. In this construct, the media's agenda reflects the priorities of policymakers, with creative roles for the media normally restricted to the "quality press," which has traditionally provided a forum for informed debate. A century-old example of this model of influence is Lord Salisbury's use of the *London Times* to float the outlines of a new British policy toward Africa.[51]

A revised and so-called popular model recognizes the importance of domestic politics, public opinion, and consequently the influence of pollsters in the policy process. Because of the vigorous interaction between the media and public opinion, the popular model also assumes greater influence on the part of television, radio, and tabloid journalism. This latter model, epitomized by the term *CNN factor,* suggests a reversal of policy-media effect, with a consequent loss of control by government policymakers to the media.[52]

The CNN effect: surely it exists, and surely we went to Somalia and Rwanda partly because of its magnetic pull.
—General Shalikashvili chairman, U.S. Joint Chiefs of Staff[53]

These two models of media-policy interaction can also be applied to the other sides of the crisis triangle. Regarding media-humanitarian interaction, the traditional model would be that the media simply report; the popular model would be that the media coverage influences the course of such activities. Regarding humanitarian-policy interaction, the traditional view would be that aid activities follow the flag of donor nations. The revised view would underscore the reality that humanitarian activities influence the foreign policies and perceived national interests of the donor governments. As with media interaction with policymaking, the post–Cold War era has enlivened the triangular interaction considerably and altered the traditional patterns of dominance and subservience.

Generally speaking, research literature and case examples support conclusively neither the traditional nor the popular model. Passions run high and views are ardently defended, but there is no real dichotomy between media-dictated policy and policy-dictated media. Nor can humanitarian action be seen as dictated by either the media or government policymakers. The interplay is fluid and dynamic; the experience is rich and diverse.

Media-linked international action responding to humanitarian crises is not just a post–Cold War phenomenon. Television pictures of starving children in Biafra in 1968 are credited with provoking a major response,

T<i>he effect of the press is in general more substantial in foreign policy than in domestic policy. We are not at all sure why this is so, or what are the consequences for both of the specific differences.*
—Martin Lipsky[56]

primarily NGO-led, and with sparking the creation of Médecins Sans Frontières.[54] The Burke-Amin coverage of the 1984 Ethiopian famine, televised first in Britain and subsequently in the United States, is universally cited as the trigger for a massive popular reaction and concomitant international response. But events of the 1990s have accelerated the process described by the former head of the French chapter of Médecins Sans Frontières Rony Brauman as the enshrining of "the victim and his rescuer [as] one of the totems of our age."[55]

CASE STUDIES

These cases represent a cross-section of post–Cold War crises and exhibit varying degrees of coverage by the media, attention by government policymakers, and action by humanitarian organizations. Since the cases fit no simple classification scheme, they are presented roughly in chronological order.

Questions to be addressed in each case include:

1. Phases: What were the key phases of the involvement of each of the institutions that make up the crisis triangle? How did the crisis emerge and move across these various phases? Did the institutions share a common timetable, or did each follow its own agenda?

2. Links: How did the three institutions of the crisis triangle interact? What were the discernible links among media coverage, policymaking, and humanitarian responses? What were the dominant factors in the interactive process? Did one institution assume and maintain leadership throughout?

3. Results: What were the outcomes of the interaction for each of the three institutions? What was the extent of influence by the news media on the processes of policy formation and humanitarian action? To what extent can effective responses in one crisis form the basis for future actions in other settings?

Liberia: An Obscure Crisis, a Limited Response

Despite widespread violence and suffering over more than five years, the Liberian civil war has received sparse international coverage and exhibits little media-policy interaction. The lack of engagement by external media paralleled international disinterest; it is not apparent which was cause and which was effect. International diplomatic response was limited to support for a regional intervention by the Economic Community of West African States (ECOWAS) and a belated UN political initiative. International humanitarian organizations provided assistance from the inception of civil strife, in December 1989, at levels of per capita largesse disproportionate to the sparse news media attention paid to the crisis.[57]

Liberia's lack of strategic profile for Western states was scarcely questioned. As the war spread in 1990, carrying with it devastating humanitarian consequences, the international community was preoccupied with radical changes in Eastern Europe and, beginning in August, the crisis in the Gulf sparked by Iraq's invasion of Kuwait. During the following year the disintegration of Yugoslavia combined with the Gulf War and the related refugee problems to eclipse events in Liberia. During 1992 and throughout 1993, Somalia joined Bosnia in the international limelight. In mid-1994, Rwanda temporarily took center stage. Across this half-decade, Liberia's bloodletting continued virtually unabated in an obscure war well beyond the purview of the international community.

Ironically, the scale of suffering in Liberia matched or exceeded the distress in conflicts that commanded greater media coverage. Liberia's entire population of 2.5 million was affected, with 1.8 million dependent on humanitarian aid by 1995.[58] The UN reported in early 1995 150,000 casualties, 865,000 refugees, 800,000 internally displaced persons. The population of Monrovia swelled to 1.3 million, nearly three times the prewar level. The international view of Liberia, which rivalled many other complex emergencies not only in terms of human suffering but also in the degree of state collapse, was obscured by external coverage and policy attention paid to Bosnia, Somalia, and even southern Sudan.

Physical access was not an insoluble problem for reporters. From the outset, the BBC World Service radio and a group of agency reporters based in Abidjan maintained a steady stream of news—which was little disseminated or used outside the region. But visits by foreign television crews were infrequent, with headline news reserved for the most extreme violence—among such events were the massacre of civilians who had sought refuge in churches, in July 1990, and the renewed assault on the capital of Monrovia, in October 1992. The Liberian conflict "was reported as a weird, lower-order war," said an NGO press officer, reflecting on his unsuccessful efforts to call greater attention to the mayhem. The international media ventured into Liberia, it appears, to provide bizarre documentary-style coverage from the "Heart of Darkness" rather than news of a serious threat to international peace and security.[59]

The Liberian media played a vigorous but highly partisan role. Humanitarian agencies attempted to use local news services to publicize the details of aid operations in a climate where mistrust and rumor often derailed impartial operations. The local media, captive to various Liberian factions, were never a reliable source of news. External media were therefore a crucial source of objective information for all participants.[60]

The situation seemed to have the makings of a higher priority crisis for both the United States and the European Union. Close historical ties—Liberians call themselves "children of America"—led many in the West African country to expect, and to advocate, U.S. military intervention. A sizable, articulate, and politically active population of Liberian-Americans and Liberian refugees in the United States did its best to increase the scale of Washington's interest and involvement. Stirrings of a foreign policy based more clearly on support for human rights and market democracies were also elements in Liberia's favor. Yet such factors failed to produce a more active U.S. policy response. Likewise, the European Union and its member states restricted their own level of policy attention and response largely to that of providing humanitarian aid.

Generally free of media or public pressure to produce instant solutions, Western policymakers had an opportunity to develop long-term strategies. But their reactions were shaped by a narrow view of Liberia's geopolitical relevance, and, although Liberia was on the agenda of specialized aid officials, it never attained much political visibility. Washington's support for ECOMOG, the West African peacekeeping force, was cautious. In both the United States and the European Union, the policy response focused on short-term support of the humanitarian agencies, with humanitarian aid used more as a palliative than an integral part of a comprehensive strategy.

Liberia was not alone in the category of ignored crises. In Sudan there was a similar lack of international resolve to address the issues raised by the protracted civil war between the secessionist Sudan People's Liberation Army (SPLA) and the Islamic government in Khartoum. In the 1990s, that war, which had been more or less ongoing since the Sudan received its independence in the mid-1950s, produced a humanitarian crisis that, in numbers of persons affected, exceeded either the Kurdish or Somali emergencies. Despite "casualties and displacement of people by the million," noted one commentator, the United Nations "has chosen to regard it as a strictly internal matter."[61] Sporadic media coverage of events in the Sudan did little to change its relative lack of priority.

The Sudan suffers from perennial lack of attention (Coverage of the Sudan was inhibited by access problems due to geography and logistics, poor communications, visa complications, and safety concerns.)[62] Like the conflicts in Angola, Afghanistan, and Liberia, the protracted war in the Sudan received coverage only at moments of high violence, visibly calamitous suffering, or political crisis. "Sudan is evidence of the starving baby syndrome," said one commentator, referring to the media's tendency to cover only highly visible crises, "where only peaks of suffering during a 13-year war have merited coverage."[63] Such peaks in 1989 and 1993 produced surges of pressure to do something to reduce starvation, followed by flurries of humanitarian diplomacy to gain access to the affected populations.

Humanitarian agencies have made attempts to publicize these forgotten crises. Coalitions of organizations, particularly in the United Kingdom and the United States, have monitored developments closely, employing the considerable information available from humanitarian and journalistic circles.[64] Humanitarian groups focusing on the problems of aid distribution and human rights abuse have enjoyed some short-term successes, but the diplomatic démarches they have supported have failed to end the wars or bring durable solutions to the plight of civilians. Ironically, such countries as Liberia, Angola, and Sudan depend upon dramatic deterioration of humanitarian conditions to increase the likelihood of media coverage and international attention.

These forgotten crises form a baseline for assessing the affect of media coverage on public policy and humanitarian action. Liberia and the Sudan, for example, have received relatively high per capita levels of humanitarian aid from the United States and other major donors, largely irrespective of media coverage. Afghanistan and Angola, which were perceived as front-line states in the global struggle between communism and capitalism and had received ample coverage and generous aid in earlier days, have received less of each in the post–Cold War era.

Northern Iraq: Providing Comfort in an Emerging Televised Order

The deployment of coalition troops in northern Iraq in April 1991 to create "safe havens" for Kurds was viewed at the time as heralding a new era of humanitarian intervention, with television leading the charge. "Television coverage of wretched Kurds dying in freezing mountains day after day aroused huge sympathy from international public opinion," observed Médecins Sans Frontières, leading Western capitals to put "rising pressure on the White House."[65] The impacts were confirmed by those involved in policymaking. "I do think the vividness of television images probably heightened the sense of urgency," noted U.S. Under-Secretary of Defense Paul Wolfowitz. "The inescapable fact was that you had a half a million [Kurdish] people who, if nothing was done, were liable to all die and start dying rather quickly."[66]

Pictures of the massive Kurdish exodus, involving two million people—a scale of displacement comparable to Rwanda in 1994—undoubtedly moved public opinion and impelled humanitarian action. In the United Kingdom, the public response to an initial appeal from aid groups for contributions exceeded $3 million. The British government's decision to participate in the initiative to create "save havens" for refugees, however, was triggered by domestic political factors rather than by the pressure of public opinion: Sources close to the decisionmaking process noted that Prime Minister John Major feared criticism for inaction from his predecessor Margaret Thatcher, who had taken it upon herself to meet with Kurdish refugee leaders in an effort to goad her government to act.

At the international level, the protection of the Kurds was regarded as the "next episode" in the Gulf War, which already had featured dramatic footage of the rout of Iraqi forces by coalition troops. The allies had controlled the media effectively in their victory; the media, using television as the main source, provided the vital link between events and Western publics. "But the military supplied much of the news that came out of the Gulf through briefings and videotapes," concluded one study. "Therefore what Americans saw on their screens reflected the government's viewpoint."[67] Televised pictures of Kurdish refugees massed along the Turkish border built on a Western consensus that an obligation to them existed, growing out of the stand already taken against Iraq. In fact, their continued distress and repression threatened the political dividends to be reaped from a successful Gulf War.[68]

Following authorization in April 1991 by the Security Council, coalition troops invaded northern Iraq from Turkey, reclaiming land occupied by the Iraqi army north of the thirty-sixth parallel to which the Kurds sought to return. The well-televised establishment of safe havens demonstrated that the coalition forces could maintain their subjugation of Iraqi leader Saddam Hussein. An additional consideration from Turkey's point of view was the need to prevent refugees from crossing the border to join an already troublesome and destabilizing Kurdish population inside Turkey. Media-generated pressure thus built upon events to reinforce a rationale for what was widely described as a "humanitarian intervention." The Kurds were already high on the agenda of policymakers, but the media helped frame a new imperative for action.

The actual intervention, involving 10,000 American, British, French, and Dutch troops, was short-lived. Of the three safe havens, the U.S.-controlled sector received the most media attention because it was the easiest to access and had large refugee camps. Moreover, the U.S. military were skilled in handling the media, which were part of a strategy both as an additional means of protection for the refugees and to give the humanitarian operation credibility. "The tensions were practically nonexistent" between the military and the media, reported U.S. General John M. Shalikashvili, "and we not only were able to give the press total freedom to roam the operations area, but we gave them maximum support to get around and be better informed. The result was a more factual story filed, a better-informed public, a better-informed Washington, and thus better support for us in the field."[69]

By July 1991, the presence of coalition troops had been replaced by air cover, which was sufficient to keep Baghdad at bay. The media departed as quickly as the troops, with some passing depiction of the handover of humanitarian activities to the United Nations and cooperating nongovernmental organizations. With no political settlement in place that would guarantee the security of the Kurds, however, the Iraqi government resumed pressure on them, obstructing and harassing humanitarian activities, in direct contravention of agreements between Iraq and the United Nations.

Attempts by humanitarian organizations and by the Kurds themselves, both in the region and in Europe and North America, to maintain media interest ran against the tide of events. Both the sanctions and the NATO air watch remained in effect, but international resolve to protect and assist the newly resettled refugees no longer had the same profile. Among the factors that made the story more difficult to tell were public divisions among Kurdish leadership regarding the political future of the area, the embargo imposed from Baghdad on relief supplies and fuel bound for the north, and, as time went by, the Iraqi refusal to comply with the detailed provisions of UN Security Council resolutions following the war.

As the continuing humanitarian plight of the Kurds in northern Iraq ebbed in visibility, some aid workers expressed a concern that international fear of Kurdish self-determination had now replaced fear of Kurdish extermination. The international community was no longer receiving the kind of headline news coverage reserved for the earlier crisis and for military intervention—the media were following the lead of policymakers much as they had in the course of the Gulf War. (Those close connections resulted in post-mortems about issues of journalistic independence and media access during war situations.)

Humanitarian agencies were sidelined for much of the early crisis by the advent and presence of the military, which brought a unique security and logistic capability to the task of assisting civilians affected by the conflict. For the American military, it was the first of a new breed of large-scale humanitarian missions that generated experience and enthusiasm for subsequent operations. For aid groups, the experience was also a first. It taught them how to collaborate with the military and eventually, as troops withdrew, to assume greater responsibilities themselves.

In the United Kingdom, a contributing factor in the marginalization of aid groups was the campaigning activity of a populist politician, Jeffrey Archer, whose efforts resulted in the mobilization of media attention and relief funding from numerous sources. This high-profile push caused acute embarrassment for NGOs, many of whom were intent on keeping attention on Africa but felt obliged to join in both the fundraising and subsequent activities in Iraq. As a result, NGO influence over policymaking processes and resource mobilization both directly and through the media were considerably reduced.

As of late 1995, the welfare of the Iraqi Kurds remained fragile, although NATO air cover was keeping Saddam Hussein from attacking them and other UN sanctions to pressure the Baghdad regime remained in place. Headline news was again written in April and May of 1995 in the wake of a Turkish invasion to counter Kurd nationalist forces, but without stimulating much debate on long-term prospects. In short, the media and humanitarian action assumed tactical importance at a specific stage in the crisis, but were less significant in the long term compared with regional and internal Kurdish politics.

Somalia: The Push–Pull of Television

The impact of news media on foreign policy is illustrated often by reference to Somalia. It is argued that the news media drove the erratic course of international response to both the collapse of the state and the people's suffering. Television news is singled out as the main stimulus in the process, supposedly triggering Washington's military intervention and then its abrupt withdrawal. According to the chairman of a congressional committee: "Pictures of the starving children, not policy objectives, got us into Somalia in 1992. Pictures of U.S. casualties, not the completion of our objectives, led us to exit Somalia."[70] A review of events, however, indicates that the crisis passed through several phases during which media involvement and policy formation had far less clear-cut correlation.[71]

As Somalia slipped into anarchy in 1991–1992, there was general but by no means uniform neglect from all three sides of the crisis triangle. "The lack of interest from the media, central government, and humanitarian agencies created a vacuum of advocacy or support," said one commentator, "which USAID and OFDA did not fill."[72] The response in Europe followed a similar pattern.[73]

Building to a crescendo during 1992, pressure from an increasingly well-organized lobby of concerned humanitarian agencies, policymakers, and politicians struggled to obtain appropriate attention to the deteriorating situation from both governments and the media. As of July 1992, some increase in policy and media attention on both sides of the Atlantic was evident. "By summer, a lot had been shown and written about Somalia; some of it was clear, insightful, powerful," said one observer. "But reporting never reached that critical mass. No coherent line emerged so that people far away might pay sustained attention."[74]

The onset of a U.S. military airlift of aid from neighboring Kenya brought the expected troop-following media coverage, raising Somalia's profile. In fact, that had been one of the explicit objectives of intensifying the existing airlift from one which used civilian aircraft under commercial contract to one involving military pilots and aircraft.[75] Keith Richburg of the *Washington Post,* who covered the military airlift, and then stayed on to monitor the Somalia situation, is said to have "made a difference" in attracting greater attention to the crisis.[76] In any event, Somalia finally, if belatedly, gained media—especially television—attention, becoming a story about conflict and famine in the "new world disorder." Ironically, when U.S. ground troops landed in Mogadishu in December 1992, the worst of the famine had passed and the most vulnerable already had died.[77]

From its pretext in the predictable images of starvation and civil war, "technicals" and "khat" through the saturation coverage of the "live" landing and the periodic photo opportunities that culminated in President Bush's New Year's visit and the springtime return of the troops to President Clinton's White House, to the gradual disintegration of the United Nations mission in the summer and fall, the Somalia operation has been conceptualized, practiced, and evaluated—by all parties—strictly in terms of the publicity value of the images and headlines it might produce.
—Thomas Keenan[78]

Why the turn-around in attention and action? Many observers held that a "herd instinct" had overtaken the media, each outlet concerned about being scooped by the competition. But other factors also were clearly at work. The observation in July 1992 by the UN Secretary-General that Somalia was the victim of the highly-publicized "rich man's war" in the former Yugoslavia stung governments. A small cadre of European- and U.S.-based humanitarian agencies used first-hand accounts from Somalia in a relentless campaign for greater international attention to the crisis. In the United States, certain members of Congress and administration officials (particularly in USAID) raised the political temperature of the story.

Somalia surfaced as an issue in the presidential campaign when the Bush administration was criticized by the Clinton campaign for not doing enough. "Sustained media coverage of the anarchy and starvation certainly contributed mightily to the Bush administration's decision to use U.S. troops to protect the relief effort," noted an official close to the decisionmaking process.[79]

Senior U.S. administration officials concurred on the importance of the media's role. "Television had a great deal to do with President Bush's decision to go in," reported then-Secretary of State Lawrence Eagleburger. "I was one of those two or three that was strongly recommending he do it, and it was very much because of the television pictures of these starving kids, substantial pressures from the Congress that come from the same source, and my honest belief that we could do this . . . at not too great a cost and, certainly, without any great danger of body bags coming home."[80] The role of the media notwithstanding, the domestic political context on which the media played also provided a key element in understanding the decision to commit troops. Washington, like most other Western capitals, was embarrassed over inaction in Bosnia. President Bush's own personal determination was also indispensable.[81]

Once committed to intervention, policymakers sought media approbation. As the *International Herald-Tribune* stated, "the arrival of troops in the early morning hours was perfectly timed to reach the afternoon peak television audience in the U.S., and hundreds of well-briefed reporters were on the beach and at the port."[82] The *Guardian* newspaper, referring to the need to win over U.S. domestic opinion, noted that "Media complicity in the shot-free and artificially-lighted night invasion was an essential element for the mission to succeed."[83] Indeed, the media-military cooperation extended well after the invasion. The military provided the media with security and logistics. The media reciprocated with publicity for domestic consumption and useful intelligence about conditions in the interior of the country.

However, that symbiosis changed dramatically in the summer of 1993 as security worsened and humanitarian operations faltered. Media coverage of the growing insecurity may have contributed to the pressure that something be done about the strongman Aidid. Following deadly attacks on foreign journalists in July and September, reporting became perilous and close to impossible.[84] While no American media witnessed the ill-fated Ranger raid in October 1993, the news coverage from other outlets— for once, not real time—had rapid and enormous domestic political impact. Having influenced military engagement, the media also spurred withdrawal.

Network broadcasts of Somali video pictures showing dead U.S. marines being dragged ignominiously through the streets of Mogadishu at the very least hastened—and perhaps also drove—a policy reversal by the administration. According to National Security Adviser Anthony Lake, "the [television] pictures helped us recognize that the military situation in Mogadishu had deteriorated in a way that we had not frankly recognized."[85] Reinforcing the reassessment, "thousands of phone calls to Capitol Hill demanding that America withdraw its troops . . . led to intense Congressional pressure on President Clinton."[86] A policy that had evolved from creating a safe environment for humanitarian aid to arresting noncooperative warlords then received rapid and radical revision by the White House, with a specific deadline and countdown for U.S. military withdrawal.

Analysts have stressed that the negative effect of the coverage was due not only to faulty policy formulation but also to poor communications strategy. According to one commentator, "U.S. policymakers and military leaders failed to convey to the public the reasons for shifting U.S. goals and missions." In his view, "Media stories failed to link the complexities of U.S.-UN disagreements, Somali warlord politics, tensions between military peacekeepers and nongovernmental aid organizations (many vigorously pacifist), and shifting U.S. missions."[87] Without fuller explanation and justification for the mission, any policy other than withdrawal was likely to face wide domestic condemnation and political fallout in the midterm elections in November 1994.

By this stage, the Somalia crisis also had taken on added strategic importance as a test case for U.S.-UN relations. At issue was how much Washington was prepared to police the new world order or, more technically speaking, the terms of U.S. engagement in multilateral undertakings. The immediate impact of the Somalia debacle was the prompt articulation of an exit strategy. The longer-term effect was a revision of U.S. peacekeeping criteria, finalized in May 1994 in Presidential Decision Directive (PDD) 25. These criteria narrowed future U.S. involvement in such undertakings and also restricted approval of UN efforts underwritten by Washington in which U.S. troops were themselves not involved.

In contrast to northern Iraq, the role of humanitarian agencies and NGOs in particular was pivotal. Nongovernmental organizations and the International Committee of the Red Cross (ICRC), which constituted the only international presence in Somalia after the withdrawal of the UN at the peak of the famine in 1992, formed the core humanitarian lobby. These organizations were crucial in getting the media into Somalia on relief flights, providing local transport, accommodation, communications, and, invariably, security. They also provided a national point of reference for the media. British media reported regularly on Save-the-Children (UK), the Irish media featured Concern, and the U.S. media focused on CARE. Some agencies felt exploited, however, especially when reporting did not give them the expected profile or concentrated on what they felt were wrong or unhelpful images.

Headline news tracked the U.S. military withdrawal from Somalia in the spring of 1994 and the withdrawal of UNOSOM II troops in March 1995. Somalia's subsequent decline into mid-1992 conditions has received little more attention than the first time around.

In sum, the correlation between media attention on the one hand, and action by policymakers and humanitarian agencies on the other, followed a series of peaks and valleys. At some stages, media interest (itself reflecting goading by aid actors) preceded policy initiatives; on other occasions, media involvement followed. Sequence, however, was not necessarily indicative of causation, nor was any one institution in total control of the process. Within governments, control of the policy process shifted as different levels and institutions became involved. The interaction is better understood as the interplay of two complex systems—not of unitary actors—with media impact dependent upon on other variables in domestic and international politics.

The media were not fully autonomous actors in Somalia, dependent as they were at different times on aid agencies and taking their cues from the military. Yet they enjoyed enough freedom of action to make a difference at crucial points in the process and to influence the process itself. Television in particular played a crucial role. One commentator finds the lesson of Somalia to be that "No story lives long without TV coverage."[88]

Former Yugoslavia:
Blanket Coverage, Selective Action

Despite virtually continuous news coverage of the conflicts since the beginnings of the break-up in 1991, the media seems not to have had a major impact on the strategic policy of Western governments. The determination of policymakers in Europe to insulate the rest of Europe from a local crisis and in the United States to avoid the commitment of troops before a peace agreement successfully resisted all pressure for a more engaged approach.

Peace initiatives late in the summer of 1995—which did mark a basic change that led to the Dayton accords—reflected political opportunities created by a changed military situation on the ground rather than a media-inspired change of policy direction. Although various forms of NATO and UN action were debated and tried, peace enforcement was never a serious policy option. UN peacekeeping forces concentrated on noncombative and humanitarian missions rather than engaging in the more coercive action that the invocation of authority under Chapter VII of the UN Charter permitted. "Collective spinelessness" rather than "collective security" was the policy.[89]

Strategic policy has proved largely immune from media influence, but peaks of shocking news coverage, particularly from Bosnia, have produced heightened international reactions that have influenced the tactics used by governments and the United Nations. Security Council Resolution 770 of 1992 supported humanitarian aid. Subsequent U.S. air-drops of aid, emergency medical evacuations from Sarajevo by the UK, and even NATO's protection measures for the Bosnian capital were all responses to well-televised predicaments. In retrospect, these actions appear to have been exercises in damage control in response to public exposure of governmental impotence instead of key elements in established or evolving policy.[90] Governments wary of public criticism for inaction soon reverted to a basic reluctance to adopt stronger measures to halt ethnic cleansing or other flouting of international norms.

As former British Foreign Secretary Douglas Hurd said, "We have not been [willing], and are not willing to begin some form of military intervention, which we judge useless or worse, simply because of day-to-day pressures from the media."[91] International resolve to contain rather than confront conflict in the former Yugoslavia survived relentless pressure that at times was led by the media.[92] Neither the European Union nor the United States has been drawn into a ground war to halt atrocities, ensure humanitarian access, or enforce peace, despite graphic and comprehensive news coverage. Short-term palliatives have represented the limit of response, addressing individual problems and not root causes.

One of the clearest examples of media influence upon the tactical or presentational aspects of policy (as is distinct from underlying strategies) was the response of policymakers to the explosion of a shell in the Sarajevo marketplace in February 1994. The bloody aftermath received detailed international television coverage and was followed by a frenzy of diplomatic activity and a NATO ultimatum to Serbs to withdraw heavy artillery from the mountains around Sarajevo. However, subsequent analysis suggests that the television images, rather than creating new policy, crystallized an international consensus that was already in the making.

Acknowledging the contributory effect of the media on this occasion, U.S. Secretary of State Warren Christopher remarked, "Television images moved forward a policy we had clearly started on . . . but television should not be the sole determinant of policy."[93] The media also figured in the decision of California Senator Diane Feinstein to change her vote to favor lifting the arms embargo in July 1995. "One image punched through to me," she commented. "That young woman hanging from a tree [near Srebrenica]. That to me said it all."[94]

The case of "little Irma" Hadzimuratovic demonstrated the power of media coverage to promote specific humanitarian action. In July 1993, the plight of this young mortar victim, whose shrapnel wounds were beyond medical treatment available in Sarajevo, penetrated media and policy processes at the peak of the slow summer news season, capturing the attention of the British public and of Prime Minister John Major. The ensuing UK-led military airlift of Irma and forty other victims was condemned by some as callous and exploitative; a senior UK policymaker in an off-the-record comment described the media pressure as "irresponsible, an illegitimate use of media power." Nevertheless, though the coverage did expedite further evacuations and provoke a response from an audience numbed by two years of war coverage, there was no change in fundamental policy because of the bloodshed.

The implementation of policy decisions sometimes felt the weight of media exposure. As Major General Lewis MacKenzie, commander of UNPROFOR in Sarajevo, reported, "Wherever the media goes, a lot of serious violations of human rights either move away or stop. The media was the only major weapon system I had. Whenever I went into negotiations with the warring parties, it was a tremendous weapon to be able to say: 'OK, if you don't want to do it the UN's way, I'll nail your butt on CNN in about 20 minutes.' That worked, nine times out of ten."[95]

The media also highlighted efforts by international organizations to reach and assist civilians caught in the conflicts in the former Yugoslavia. The difficulties encountered by aid convoys made good footage and also provided western governments good televisual material to show that they were "doing something" in a climate in which they were accused of doing too little. While governments emphasized their own humanitarian role, aid agencies were calling for stronger security measures, often finding an ally in the media. The lead UN agency in the former Yugoslavia, UNHCR, was uncharacteristically outspoken in condemning human rights abuses and the obstruction of aid. Media attention undoubtedly kept pressure on governments to persevere with aid operations in the face of mounting casualties and a potential domestic political backlash. Humanitarian aid was directed occasionally to certain areas where suffering had been uncovered by the media.

The power of the indigenous media in former Yugoslavia was both a negative force that inflamed the conflict and a positive force in the cause of reconciliation. Serb, Croat, and Bosnian authorities all made cynical and brutally effective use of the media as weapons of war. Direct threats and attacks on foreign and independent media limited their power to counteract such bias. Aware of the critical influence of Western public opinion, warring factions went all out to manipulate foreign media where they could not contain them.[96]

Haiti: A Domestic Agenda, a Divided Public

For the crisis triangle in the United States, the emergency in Haiti was analogous to that in the former Yugoslavia for institutions in Europe. In policymaking and news terms, Haiti was a humanitarian crisis with strong U.S. domestic overtones. Its location within the traditional U.S. sphere of influence elevated its geopolitical importance. The threat of refugees continuing to flow into the United States kept the crisis high on the national political agenda, with the OAS and the UN also monitoring the situation closely. Humanitarian issues in the form of well-documented human rights abuses and refugee hardships put pressure on successive administrations to live up to foreign policy objectives such as the support of democracy and human rights. A synergy between policy concerns and media interest gave Haiti a high profile in the waning months of the Bush administration, in the 1992 presidential campaign, and in the early months of the Clinton presidency.

Following the ousting of President Jean-Bertrand Aristide in a military coup in September 1991, the twin issues of democracy and human rights were kept alive by the U.S. media. "Haiti didn't drop away like other humanitarian crises," noted a Washington observer.[97] Early attention to events in Haiti, including the coup, soon gave way to a focus on the "boat people." The Haitian crisis received sustained attention throughout 1992 with the advent of new leadership in the UN secretariat and, in 1993, in the White House. News coverage in 1993 focused on the Governors Island negotiations in July and on the viability of a policy that accepted nothing less than the restoration of Aristide. During this period, the debate in the media and among U.S. policymakers became polarized, reflecting the highly politicized situation in Haiti itself. Despite independent confirmation of human rights abuses by the military regime, the exiled Aristide often received very critical press coverage about his own personal qualities and conduct while in office. One senior diplomat, studying media reports closely in preparation for his new assignment in Port-au-Prince, would later recall that the radical, fiery priest portrayed in the media bore little resemblance to the political leader whom he would observe at close hand after his restoration to power.

The contribution of the media as participant was felt acutely in October 1993 when the U.S.S. *Harlan County*, intent on a more robust assertion of U.S. policy, turned away from Port-au-Prince at the sight of a hostile mob on the shore. Aware of the sensitivity of the Clinton administration immediately following the debacle in Somalia, the military regime made calculated use of CNN coverage to threaten the United States with a repeat of the Somalia experience. The de facto regime had been equally manipulative of media and policy processes in the United States—in sharp contrast to the Aristide camp, which at the outset of its exile was described as "clueless" about Washington.

Throughout 1993–1994, vigorous media coverage of the cases for and against intervention contributed to pressure on U.S. policymakers.[98] However, the steady increase in headline coverage of human rights abuses and the refugee exodus eroded the credibility of both diplomatic and sanctions policies, neither of which was proving effective. This coverage was reported to have had a personal effect on President Clinton and to have helped build the administration's case for military coercion at a time when public opinion remained "divided and malleable."[99] Public ambivalence paralleled headline coverage that focused as much, if not more, on the perceived refugee threat to the United States as on the actual dire circumstances in Haiti.

Debate in news commentary about the nature of U.S. interests was also divided. Editorials in the *Washington Post* generally supportive of Aristide were offset by columnists in the same paper who were highly skeptical of intervention. In the *New York Times*, the balance was reversed and the editorials were more critical. With policy in flux, the media and public opinion exerted a push-pull influence. As a senior State Department adviser put it, the administration policy review of May 1994 reasserting sanctions "was driven as much as anything by criticism from media and Congress." A well thought-out political strategy on the part of the administration was not available to buffer policy from these pressures.[100]

Once the decision for military intervention had been made, the administration changed from reacting to the media to attempting to manage it. At an operational level this had mixed results. An attempt by the Pentagon to control coverage of the occupation through the pool system broke down. There were too many journalists already on the island, and events moved too quickly for the pool to keep up. Subsequent relationships with the media were easier. "All major U.S. networks," reported General Shalikashvili, "had agreed to use night vision devices and to delay broadcasting for some time after the troops were safely on the ground." Once the troops were on the ground, he added, "we received, with very few exceptions, excellent press, and the operation and the country benefited."[101] Military-media relations resembled those in northern Iraq rather than Somalia.

In building the case for military intervention, human rights organizations were more instrumental than aid agencies. The testimonies of the UN civilian observers provided an objective focus for news reports and increased coverage about human rights abuses by the de facto authorities. One UN observer felt the print media did a better job of covering the crisis, largely through use of long-term contacts and people in hiding to provide depth for their stories, rather than through the electronic media. CNN, however, infuriated the human rights community by interviewing those not afraid to speak out—that is, persons who were inevitably backers of the regime. The media were also the first to pick up on tensions between UN human rights staff and senior diplomats, who, it was feared, might compromise human rights concerns in the interests of negotiating a political solution.

Following the expulsion of UN human rights observers in July 1994, there was pressure on the remaining humanitarian aid agencies to act as the "eyes and ears" of the international community, a role to which they reacted with caution. Mindful of the media's potential, the United Nations Development Programme (UNDP) in Haiti quickly recruited a media relations specialist. In practice, this strategy was more about limiting damage than about establishing a coherent public information profile to reflect policy. With the launching of Operation Uphold Democracy, the U.S. media focused on the street activity of the U.S. military, leaving the European media to pick up on major aid stories, such as the ransacking of aid warehouses.

Some of the generic criticisms of the media as an institution already noted in Chapter 1 also were directed toward its activities in Haiti. "The U.S. media by and large covered the 'plight' of the elites in Port-au-Prince much more thoroughly than that of the rest of the country," noted an observer. The elites were more accessible, spoke English, and had little fear of retribution from the military government—but represented only a small minority of public opinion. The media were faulted also for referring to pro-Aristide crowds as "mobs" while describing paramilitaries and others paid to be on hand at the army headquarters at the time of the Carter negotiations as "demonstrators."

The Haiti emergency presents a rich illustration of the crisis triangle in action.[102] The news media played a variety of roles. A seasoned observer noted that "When Haiti turned out not to be a bloody war, senior correspondents of U.S. networks and newspapers didn't stick around." In stark contrast with the five hundred or more media personnel on hand in September 1994 at the time of the landing of the U.S.-led multinational force, only a handful were present in February 1996 to witness the democratic transfer of power at the inauguration of Aristide's successor.

The policy debate in the United States was influenced by a range of institutions, including the *Miami Herald*, National Public Radio, right-wing talk radio, and a steady drumbeat of commentators and pundits, although the nature and extent of this influence remains conjectural. Dramatic television footage of the Haitian army paramilitary group FRAPH against Aristide supporters—as portrayed in the cover photo of this book —is widely held to have influenced changes in U.S. policy, enabling troops to play a more assertive role in maintaining law and order and protecting Aristide supporters. Within Haiti, perceptions of events were influenced by the U.S. Information Service and the Voice of America.

Rwanda: A Media Blitz and an Aid Crusade

The Rwanda crisis was more akin to Somalia than to the other emergencies reviewed so far. As in Somalia, the media's impacts on government policy and humanitarian action were ostensibly more important and direct than elsewhere. As in Somalia, those impacts already have been the subject of several analyses—which are characterized by the same caution in delineating causes and effects that characterizes our own review of the media's roles.

For government policymakers, humanitarian organizations, and the news media alike, the Rwanda crisis became the most severe test of institutional capacity to respond effectively in the post–Cold War world. All three sets of institutions saw a gap in their understandings of the nature of the Rwandan conflict; all responded in relatively superficial fashion, each failing to address the underlying causes of the crisis.

Media attention, international policy formulation, and humanitarian responses moved through several phases. Before April 1994, the warning signs of impending conflict went largely unreported and unheeded by all three institutions. From April to June, genocide within Rwanda received only partial coverage and thoroughly inadequate response from policymakers and aid groups. The mass refugee exodus to Zaire in July and the ensuing cholera crisis, well-covered by the media, received a massive response from government decisionmakers and humanitarian organizations alike. By late 1994 and into 1995, when media coverage tapered off, the profile of the crisis for policymakers and humanitarian agencies also was reduced. In that phase, however, the media articulated some of the policy dilemmas raised by the crisis and response. Each phase requires closer review.

Late in 1993 and early in 1994, dire warnings by human rights and aid agencies inside and outside of Rwanda were ignored. Throughout 1993, there were clear signs of escalating regional violence emanating from Burundi, where the deaths of up to 250,000 people went largely unnoticed by media and policymakers alike.[103] During "the first three months of 1994," reported one review, "there was virtually no Western media coverage of events in Rwanda. In the early part of the year, the main African story was the UN withdrawal from Somalia, which would prove prescient in itself" for UN peacekeeping troops in Rwanda.[104] With international media absent, local media were instrumental in spreading propaganda and ultimately fueling violence.

In the immediate aftermath of the plane crash that killed the presidents of Rwanda and Burundi and unleashed a carefully prepared campaign of genocide, few news accounts kept the outside world apprised of developments. The two international journalists in Kigali on April 6 were joined by a few others who stopped en route home from the inauguration of Nelson Mandela on May 10, an event witnessed by an estimated 500 journalists. The ranks of journalists in Rwanda proper in the early months of the crisis were limited not only by the low priority attached by the media to the story but also by the prevailing insecurity. The UN peacekeeping operation, which had assumed responsibility for protecting journalists, "limited the numbers to just six or seven at any one time because of the difficult conditions and lack of resources. The lack of security meant that live, satellite broadcasting facilities were not established in the city of [Kigali] until late May."[105]

Early reporting of the Rwanda crisis contained numerous inaccuracies, demonstrating the weaknesses of "parachute reporting," the technique of dropping news teams into unfamiliar terrain. The relative absence of news personnel on the ground in Rwanda and Burundi contributed to the general lack of understanding of the dynamics of the situation. For external head-line news, the conflict was rapidly and automatically characterized as a tribal, Hutu-versus-Tutsi struggle for power, and focused during the early stages on the evacuation of French, Belgian, and other expatriates who were fleeing the bloodbath.

If government policymakers had a more sophisticated understanding of the conflict, they did little to challenge the media depiction of an an-cestral tribal struggle that surpassed the capacity of external powers to in-fluence. With "historical feud" explanations giving governments a wel-come cover for inaction, domestic political contexts determined overall policy response more than media pressure or public opinion. The conflict had elements involving both civil war and ethnic strife. But had the media been clearer from the outset in identifying its genocidal core, coverage might have reduced the convenient excuse that governments enjoyed.

Contrasting sharply with the inattention and low priority of the media early on, the mass exodus of refugees into Goma in July attracted a surge of headline news and television coverage and an overwhelming humani-tarian response. The coverage and the response accelerated with the onset of the refugee camp cholera epidemic. The refugee events not only in-volved drama and human interest but also had a simplicity and accessibil-ity that earlier developments had lacked.

The need for simplification was something that American television reporters saw as essential for any Rwanda piece which would meet the cri-teria applied by editors. "Television needs to take something complex and strip the complexity out of it," said one U.S. television reporter in ex-plaining the attractiveness of Goma stories to her editors. "For a U.S. au-dience," she added, "you have to find the qualities that make the refugees the same [as viewers] to explain the difference." A colleague confirmed that the story had to be a version of "refugees are good people to whom bad things are happening." Close observers of the Goma crisis felt the print media were more successful than the electronic media in reflecting the complexities of the situation.

The July cholera outbreak in Goma provided the ingredients for a more straightforward "innocents in hell" story and for a domestic angle. In Ireland, where RTE carried daily live broadcasts of the Irish aid agencies at work in Goma a massive \$12 million in donations were forthcoming from a public of only two million.[106] Israeli television told the story of Rwanda by concentrating on the Israeli Defense Forces medical team. Eurovision set up satellite feed facilities for broadcast to over thirty member states. U.S. media highlighted efforts by U.S. troops in Operation Support Hope to set up a water purification system.

Media coverage tapered off in the waning months of 1994 and, with the exception of the violence in May 1995, at the Kibeho camp for internally displaced persons, remained at a low level throughout 1995. One factor in the downturn was the completion of tours of duty by many soldiers of the national military contingents, leaving at year's end only the UN peacekeepers, who in their own right never attracted much publicity. Another factor was the impasse in repatriation that had developed, with refugees reluctant to return to their homes (or intimidated by Hutu elements from doing so) and the Kigali authorities not in a position to guarantee safety and due process for those venturing back. A third was the fact that Bosnia was again prominent, first with military successes by Croatia and the Bosnian government, then with successful efforts to secure a peace agreement, and finally with the deployment of 60,000 soldiers as part of the NATO-led Implementation Force (IFOR) to foster reconstruction and reconciliation.

Reviewing the influence of the media on government policy across these various phases, it is clear that the two moved in parallel. It is less clear, however, whether more media coverage early on would have produced more robust government action. U.S. policy was constrained by PDD25, and Rwanda was the first crisis in which the newly restrictive ground rules, reflecting the debacle in Somalia, were applied. U.S. officials from the president down, reported the *Washington Post*, agreed "that Rwanda simply did not meet any test for direct U.S. military involvement."[107] Televised pictures of the pandemonium in Goma accelerated the decision to press U.S. troops into service. The troops were on their way before the Pentagon's advance mission had completed its work.

European governments at the outset were equally restrained in their responses. France alone took a more assertive approach, deploying military forces in southwest Rwanda in late June. Rather than reflecting pressure from French or European media, however, *Opération Turquoise* was more the product of French political interests in Francophone Africa. As one analyst observed, the French president, who has extraordinary latitude in foreign policy, did not need encouragement from the media or the public to act.[108]

Reviewing the influence of the media on humanitarian action, several tentative conclusions may be drawn. First, the media influenced the scale and the pattern of activities by emergency assistance and human rights groups. One study found that NGOs dependent on privately donated funds

*O*peration
Support
Hope:
• *More than 300 media personnel greeted the four-man task force assessment team.*
• *Media are generally in place and prepared before the first troops arrive.*
• *The media has better communications and data processing equipment than the military.*
• *The American public, Congress, and key influencers of U.S. policy receive most of their information about the military through some form of media. The support of American public is essential, and how the military is portrayed directly affects that support.*
• *Although senior civilian and military leadership understands the importance of public information through the media, operational commanders have dedicated few personnel or resources to accomplish it.*
• *Although public affairs staff and equipment is important, the best spokespeople are commanders and individual service members.*
• *The media should be allowed maximum access within operational and security considerations.*
—*"Publicizing Hope,"* findings of a U.S. military review of the operation in Rwanda[110]

tend to gravitate toward emergencies that are receiving major media coverage. Within the Rwanda emergency, humanitarian organizations tended toward activities, which attracted media coverage. Thus, "Only a limited number of agencies were prepared to work in the sanitation sector . . . , a situation that contrasted starkly with the number of agencies working in the higher-profile activities, such as establishing cholera treatment centres and centres for unaccompanied children."[109] Few agencies chose to work in areas with less media coverage, notwithstanding the greater need in these areas.

The media consequently contributed to the serious imbalance between resources committed to refugees outside Rwanda and those directed toward improving the situation for the internally displaced persons within the country. The more ample provision for those outside Rwanda compounded the difficulties of the new regime in encouraging people to return to their homes and delayed rehabilitation. Whereas the picture-fixated nature of television news coupled with portable satellite links made the Goma refugee story irresistible, later events did not lend themselves to the convenient formulas of "victims in flight" or prove as logistically accessible.

The media also influenced the action of humanitarian organizations and those who provided them with resources by its narrow and initially inaccurate framing of the issues of the conflict. In its need to simplify, "the media got Goma wrong," said an NGO press officer. Among the refugees were perpetrators as well as victims of violence, and the complex issue of guilt went unexamined. Goma "was never portrayed as what it was," commented a television reporter, "the byproduct of genocide." The framework mentioned earlier of bad things happening to good people did not do justice to the circumstances. Even reporters who attempted an in-depth look from the start at the tougher issues, including how much Hutu power structures were using refugee camps to serve as the staging ground to retake power, had difficulty in presenting the issues.[111] Moreover, like the media, many agencies settled for simplistic formulas for describing and responding to the Rwanda crisis.

As in Somalia, the news media and humanitarian agencies were dependent on each other in achieving logistical and professional objectives. But the humanitarian agencies demonstrated an increased dependence on the media that was more about fundraising than influencing policy. "It was the battle of the numbers and the t-shirts," commented a disillusioned journalist, referring to the seemingly universal quest for publicity. Agencies citing the highest numbers of victims stood a better chance of media coverage, he reported, and visibility in the media of agency logos was considered essential for domestic fundraising. The media circus that resulted, as more than one hundred agencies set up shop in Goma in the first weeks following the refugee influx, reduced the effectiveness of efforts of humanitarian agencies to run relief operations and to relate in concerted fashion to the media and policymakers.[112]

Several lessons emerge from the Rwanda experience. First, the case illustrates the dangers of relying on the news media to provide early warning or comprehensive analysis of a complex crisis as the basis for better policy and humanitarian action. Second, it confirms strong links between media coverage, especially television, and humanitarian responses. Third, the media's focus on massive relief operations around the perimeter of Rwanda obscured the failure of the international community to prevent the slaughter within the country and weakened its effort to bring justice and rehabilitation thereafter. Finally, although the interactions within the crisis triangle remain difficult to assess, similar weaknesses in each suggest the need for structural improvements and improved cooperation.

PROVISIONAL FINDINGS

The experience in these six crises suggests the broad outlines of a framework for analysis and discussion. While the early post–Cold War years may in retrospect prove formative, subsequent crises and responses will broaden the available data and permit firmer conclusions and more definitive recommendations. The provisional findings offered here are grouped according to the categories of phases, links, and responses with which this analysis began.

Phases

It is important to distinguish the stage in a crisis at which the interaction of the institutions of the crisis triangle is being assessed. Although no crisis fits precisely the policy process outlined in Chapter 1, each case reveals a generally similar pattern with respect to institutional recognition and response by Western governments.

Institutional Stages of Media Effect on Policy

Any attempt to measure the effect of the news media on government policy needs first to identify the stage of the policy process at which the effect operates. In this regard, the focus necessarily shifts among different governmental institutions as the crisis appears on different agendas. Perhaps the most detailed illustration of the interaction was provided by growing media coverage of Somalia, traced alongside the incremental ascent of the crisis on the agendas of various government officials in Washington. To the extent that comparable detail is known about other crises, media effects might follow a similar progression.

In the Somali instance, some government officials—and, for that matter, interested humanitarian agencies—sought media coverage with the specific intent of bypassing bureaucratic delays and elevating the crisis to the highest levels of government. Although analysts agree that the media, especially television, played an important role in setting agendas, the media influence on the formulation of various options and on the choice among them appears to have been less pronounced. The downswing of influence at these stages was followed by an upswing of attention to the implementation of chosen policies. In fact, government policymakers looked to the media to demonstrate the effectiveness of the courses of action selected.

This general evolution of media involvement in crises roughly parallels a typology that emerged from one of the workshops convened to guide the preparation of the present study. Participants identified four broad stages, beginning with the "discovery" of a given crisis by the media, sometimes with the help of humanitarian organizations and sometimes of government officials. The discovery of a crisis is often followed by "inundation"—the period of snowballing interest as the media, government officials, and humanitarian groups flock to the scene in an effort to be identified with the action. During a subsequent "business-as-usual" phase, all institutions go about their respective tasks in the humanitarian sphere. Finally, comes a "wind-down" of involvement as the media and government officials, and sometimes humanitarian organizations as well, move on to other crises. During the third phase, the media may seek out particular angles of the event to pursue. During the final phase, reporting often becomes more negative and trenchant.[113]

The duration of each of these phases varies according to the dynamics of a particular emergency and of violence. The northern Iraq experience tends to be remembered for the role of the media in initially highlighting the distress of Kurds in the mountains along the Turkish border,

Table 1   Humanitarian Assistance for Selected Complex Emergencies: UN Consolidated InterAgency Appeals

Affected Area	Target Beneficiaries	Requirements in UN appeal	Percentage Received[a]	Implementation Period[b]
Liberia	1,500,000	$110 million	33.8%	9/95–8/96
Iraq	1,300,000	$169 million	47.9%	4/95–3/96
Somalia	1,550,000	$ 93 million	30.3%	1/95–6/95
Former Yugoslavia	3,523,500	$515 million	89.5%	1/95–12/95
Haiti	2,220,000	$ 94 million	54.3%	12/94–5/95
Rwanda[c]	3,700,000	$668 million	91.7%	1/95–12/95

Source: UN Department of Humanitarian Affairs, "UN Consolidated Inter-Agency Humanitarian Assistance Appeals, Summary of Requirements and Contributions by Affected Country/Region for Appeals Ongoing/Launched in 1995," March 22, 1996. The figures shown are generally limited to the needs to be addressed by the United Nations and collaborating governments and NGOs. As a result, some needs may not be shown in the Requirements column and some funds not reflected in the Percentage Received column.
Notes: a. Includes carryover funds from previous appeals which were available for use during the stated period.
b. The periods of the appeals vary according to the circumstances of the various crises. In many cases, earlier appeals preceded those shown (seven, in the case of Iraq); in some cases, continuing needs were the subject of subsequent appeals. As indicated, funds requested for each emergency cover twelve month periods, with the exception of Somalia and Haiti, for which six month funding requests and receipts are shown.
c. The Rwanda figures include requirements for Rwandese in Zaire, Tanzania, Burundi, and Rwanda.

the Rwanda experience for the inundation of attention received during the Goma period, and so on. Media coverage and influence in a given crisis also may be cyclical, as demonstrated in Somalia. The staying power of the media is also often limited, as Haiti and northern Iraq suggest, with the winding down of involvement often preceding the resolution of the problems involved.

Links

Across these different stages, media impact on policy may be identified in two ways: by the level of policy at which impact occurs and by how much influence the media exercises. Experience suggests that media influence

Figure 5
Percent of Assistance Requirements Received for Selected Complex Emergencies

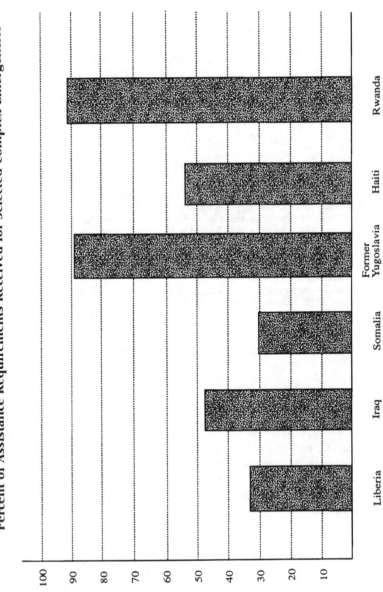

Source: UN Department of Humanitarian Affairs

on policy and humanitarian response is variable, but other factors, especially the domestic political contexts within which the media and the events that they report are situated, are at least as important in determining governmental responses. Where the media has had clear impact, television coverage has been critical.

Levels of Media Effect on Policy

Three broad levels of media effect can be discerned from recent complex emergencies. Simplified for analytical purposes, they nevertheless help to differentiate impacts at the various levels of policy formulation. Particular crises also can move across these levels as their perceived relevance to national interests changes.

• *Strategic:* The media, especially television, may have a noticeable influence on broad matters of government strategy. These include decisions on whether or not to intervene in a crisis, whether to change radically the nature of a given intervention, or whether to withdraw altogether. Intervention and withdrawal from Somalia, a more cautious approach toward Rwanda, and the military intervention in Haiti are all evidence of the influence of the news media on strategic policy in Washington. A closer analysis of these and other cases, however, reveals that other factors, such as the influence of domestic political considerations, are also at work. Likewise, interventions by the United Kingdom in northern Iraq and by the United States in Haiti demonstrate the importance in broad policy matters of crucial domestic political agendas.

• *Tactical:* At the more operational level of tactics, the news media may have a significant influence, whether or not they have played a role in the shape of the overall strategy. In Bosnia, for example, increased measures to protect Sarajevo—no-fly zones, weapons collection points, and aerial attacks—were tactical innovations that responded in part to media coverage and growing public concern. These measures became the focus of extensive media coverage, but they never challenged the overall Western strategy of avoiding a more confrontational and forcible approach.

Coverage of the aid airlift by the U.S. military from Kenya to Somalia in August 1992, itself introduced with an eye to engendering greater media and public pressure on the decisionmaking process, represented at the time a change in tactics. Yet a direct political push from the U.S. president was required before overall strategic changes occurred, spearheaded by the U.S.-led armed intervention in December. In that push, the media played a key but probably not decisive role. Preoccupation with tactics regarding Haiti also demonstrated vigorous interaction between U.S. policy and the media.

• *Presentational:* The media may stimulate cosmetic changes in policy that are designed primarily for media presentation and public consumption. In this category are such actions as medical evacuations by the British government of a small number of victims from Bosnia and the limited humanitarian response by the U.S. military in Rwanda. These kinds of action also may represent tactical responses to a given problem, but they are "presentational" in that, however constructive in their own right, they probably would not have been undertaken apart from the media exposure that would accompany them. Such measures amount to little more than photo opportunities that create difficulties in distinguishing reality from the presented image.

Degrees of Media Effect on Policy

Within each stage, level, and policymaking institution, the news media exert varying degrees of influence. In some cases they are primary movers; in others, influence may be secondary; in still others, negligible. The degrees of influence described are based on the collective judgments of participants and observers, although there is little unanimity among them.

• *Primary Effect.* In certain instances, the media dominate, control, or even supplant the usual policy processes, sidelining the normal institutions of policymaking. Examples from particular institutions at specific points, especially regarding tactical or presentational changes, include moments of policy uncertainty in Somalia, Haiti, and Rwanda that led to control shifting toward the media, especially television. Media control was also evident in the case of the UK medical evacuations from Bosnia.

Short-term actions in the humanitarian sphere appear to be closely correlated to media influence. At work here are several factors. A principal one involves the difficulty in complex emergencies of achieving consensus among or within governments on tougher and more risky political or military actions. The dramatic and photogenic nature of international actions to assist and protect besieged populations serve the interests of governments in being seen to be "doing something." Particularly attractive are the activities of foreign military forces, often to the exclusion of local actors.

Recent experience suggests that only well into crisis reportage—Rwanda provides a striking illustration—do the media ask probing questions about the underlying cause of the distress or the longer-term impacts of the government policies and actions undertaken.

• *Secondary Effect.* Only on rare occasion are the media the primary impetus to a government's course of action. More typically, the media exercise a secondary, contributory effect, often when there exists a broader policy consensus. The tendency is to stimulate short-term action with aid as a palliative rather than the vigorous and dangerous security intervention

required to enforce international decisions and norms. Humanitarian operations in northern Iraq and Bosnia had discernible links with influential
media coverage but were also the products of the overall political context—dovetailing with such overriding policy considerations as keeping
Saddam Hussein under siege and wishing to be seen "doing something."

• *Negligible Effect.* There are crises in which the media appear not to
have had much impact at all. These seem to have been situations in which
a clear strategy or expression of national interests already had been articulated, resulting in concerted government resistance to changing fundamental policy. Once intervention in Haiti was determined, fears expressed
in the media about the likelihood of limited success did not reverse policy.
Repeated British and French determination to persevere in their strict in-
terpretation of the UNPROFOR mandate was sufficient to resist pressure
either to broaden terms of engagement or to withdraw troops altogether. In
the forgotten crises of Liberia and Angola, media coverage never achieved
the critical mass necessary to have visible influence on policy processes.

Overall the essential dynamic is that the media effect on policy de-
creases as the clarity of definition and articulation of strategic interest in-
creases. "To the degree . . . that U.S. foreign policy in a given region has
been clearly stated and adequate [and] accurate information provided," observed television journalist Ted Koppel, "the influence of television coverage diminishes proportionately."[114] Other television reporters have de-
tected significant media impact "only at moments of policy panic" or
"where policymaking is weak or cynical." Although television assumed a
high profile in accounts of policy influence, closer analysis revealed an interdependence with other forms of news media.

Responses

Governmental response to humanitarian crises has clearly changed during
the early post–Cold War period. Initial willingness by governments to respond more actively, first with the intervention in northern Iraq and then in
Somalia, has been followed by greater caution in Bosnia and Rwanda.
Early experience may well have alerted policymakers also to the dangers
of overreaction to the media. Media effect on policy has become more limited, often linked to humanitarian as distinct from political or military action. Humanitarian action is likely to proceed on a case-by-case basis, with
consistent principles and practice still a matter of discussion.

Effect of the Media on Operational Courses of Action

How do the media make a difference in the choice of particular actions?
The clearest linkage is between media exposure and aid responses. For
governmental policymakers, humanitarian aid plays well in response to

headline news. Visibility is paramount; the quantity or quality of the resulting humanitarian action is less important. Greater visibility of aid was a principal objective in the formation in 1992 of ECHO. NGOs delivering aid always have had a contractual obligation to display the EU logo, and USAID supplies carry the clasped hands emblem and are marked "Gift of the People of the United States of America."

Although "foreign aid" is frequently misunderstood and sometimes unpopular with voting publics, humane impulses are firmly rooted and humanitarian action enjoys a significant constituency at peaks of visible suffering.[115] In the United States and Europe, this constituency, represented by an influential coalition of legislators and NGOs, has a powerful voice. "People in their living rooms are watching history in the making," explains Sylvana Foa, then UNHCR spokesperson. "They like it and the fact they can influence it." Aid in such circumstances may satisfy the media and public opinion agendas, but it risks becoming a palliative rather than a policy. Without appropriate political and security frameworks, aid agencies have experienced limited success. Moreover, there are growing concerns that, in crises like Rwanda, Bosnia, and the Sudan, humanitarian aid, despite short-term positive benefits, also directly and indirectly prolongs conflicts.[116]

Strategic policy, once set, is unlikely to be influenced or reversed by the media, but until it is set, the media enjoys considerable space. Furthermore, in the present geopolitical moment, the potential for media influence is heightened. As U.S. National Security Adviser Anthony Lake has commented, "It was a lot easier to think about the world in which you were trying to deal with aggression primarily across borders than [within] them."[117]

Once governments have clarified the importance of dealing with internal armed conflicts, they will have reduced the potential and the need for belated and limited media-linked responses.

Effect of the Media Within War Zones

The effect of the media within countries undergoing complex emergencies needs separate analysis. In addition, the roles of external and local media need to be distinguished. Both are increasingly recognized as key factors in the generation, continuation, and resolution of humanitarian crises, but each acts in different political contexts. Of particular concern is the use of media as a tool of diplomacy or of propaganda.

The policy impacts of external media are normally played out in far-off capitals, but they also can have a significant impact on in-country operations. As the case studies demonstrate, the external media can act as humanitarian agents, encouraging the targeting of aid toward areas of publicized need or discouraging human rights violations. In Liberia, they provided objective information at a time when indigenous communications media were thoroughly politicized. As belatedly realized in Somalia and Rwanda, those who intervene have a challenge and responsibility to disseminate accurate and current information about the nature of their activities.

The media native to conflict areas—be they local, national, or regional—are a potential force for reconciliation in civil war settings. They also may be used by humanitarian agencies to ensure greater transparency of operations. Frequently, with a focus on influencing governments and publics in donor countries, expatriates in war zones concentrate media relations efforts on western news organizations to the exclusion of indigenous channels, but for indigenous outlets to achieve their full potential, international actors need explicit strategies that nurture working relationships with them.

Local media often reflect and deepen the politicization of conflicts as the former Yugoslavia and Rwanda demonstrate. Though external media can become targets of manipulation by warring factions, where local media are thoroughly politicized, external media carry a heavier burden of responsibility to convey accurate information and to encourage reconciliation. The specific problems of propaganda and "hate radio" are the subject of separate studies.[118]

Effect of the Media on Humanitarian Action

The media have an impact on humanitarian action in high-profile crises: that impact appears to be greater than the impact of humanitarian actors on the media. The imbalance reflects a variety of factors, including the lack of coordination among humanitarian groups and the lack of individual and corporate strategies for relating to the media as an institution.

Humanitarian agencies enjoy a privileged position to influence policy processes, both directly and through the media. Their uneven success rate in doing so in part reflects variables in media-policy interaction that are beyond the control of such agencies, and in part results from structural limitations.

Coordination among humanitarian organizations is difficult, straddling, as they do, agencies in the intergovernmental, governmental, and nongovernmental arenas, each with divergent points of view. Consensus is lacking on matters such as how to ensure the security of humanitarian operations and how to relate to the increased activism of international military forces in the humanitarian sphere. NGO publicity objectives frequently are torn between collaboration as advocates and competition as fundraisers. In addition, NGOs that rely increasingly on government grants may be less willing or less able to criticize their paymasters.

The news media can sometimes be implicated in undesirable developments on the humanitarian front. Coverage of the deteriorating situation in Goma helped stimulate an enormous outpouring of resources from governments and the public. Yet it also led to increased posturing and competition among a wide array of aid groups and to the imbalance of resource allocations—to the advantage of photogenic sectors and refugees and to the detriment of Rwanda's own reconstruction agenda and internally displaced persons. The opportunism of humanitarian organizations in the circumstances has led to serious and recurring questions about their professionalism and accountability.

The capacity of the media, using the latest technology, to convey information rapidly is also exerting new pressures on humanitarian actors. Amnesty International members who see atrocities on television demand to know what their organization is doing to address them. Some personnel fear that such pressure may introduce changes in their organizational cultures. The traditional emphasis on doing what is needed—which often requires patience, nuance, and discretion—could give way to a push to do anything quick and visible.[119] The need of agencies to be perceived as in the vanguard rather than playing catch-up with media-identified crises has negative as well as positive aspects.

SUMMARY

The new world disorder has imbedded humanitarian crises in complex emergencies that have varying and yet-to-be articulated elements of national interest. In the early post–Cold War era, the international community and its principal governmental and humanitarian actors swung toward greater interventionism, sometimes with a heavy military component. More recently, they have reverted to a more isolationist mode. The news media, and television in particular, have contributed to the movements in both directions.

It is clear the media play an increasingly influential role within the international humanitarian aid system. However, for a variety of reasons it is difficult to determine precisely how influential this role is and how it varies between different contexts and between different types of agency.
—Joint Evaluation of Emergency Assistance to Rwanda[120]

Humanitarian action, whether as a concerted policy or as a substitute for more vigorous diplomacy and military intervention, has enjoyed a high profile. As a short-term measure, humanitarian action offers an effective counter to media pressure on policymakers. But for governments and humanitarian agencies, aid-only response falls short in situations in which insecurity is high and political and diplomatic objectives remain unclear. While honest scrutiny of these failings (a process in which the media also are playing a role) may weaken short-term support for humanitarian action, it also may contribute over the longer term to the effectiveness of such action.

The experience of recent years, and these provisional findings assessing the interactions within the crisis triangle, offer several suggestions to improve coverage by the news media, policy by governments, and action by humanitarian organizations. These are the subject of Chapter 3.

Figure 6
Public Opinion and the Crisis Triangle

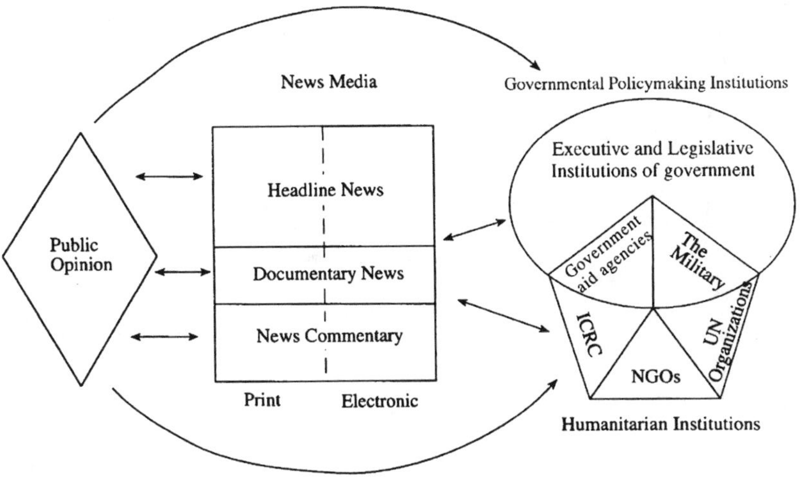

Arrows represent key lines of influence suggested by case studies in Chapter Two.
Note the disproportionate influence of Headline News.

Chapter Three

Common Ground for Improvement: Better Policy, Better Action, Better Coverage

This chapter proposes ways in which each set of institutions can function more effectively in the humanitarian sphere and achieve greater cooperation with the others while not losing sight of its own primary objectives. Functioning more effectively is valuable in its own right; enhanced cooperation does not necessarily mean a loss of integrity or independence. The news media increasingly function as a humanitarian actor. The assumption is not that its agenda should become exclusively humanitarian but that its current contribution to effective humanitarian action can be enhanced.

Three sets of recommendations address policymakers, humanitarian organizations, and the news media and identify for each the context in which that institution will need to function and the areas in which accountability needs to be improved. Reflecting the view that governments carry the preeminent responsibility for responding to complex emergencies, the contribution of each of the actors to better policy is highlighted. A concluding section frames more general recommendations for all three institutions.

RECOMMENDATIONS FOR
GOVERNMENT POLICYMAKING INSTITUTIONS

The Future Policy Context

There is not yet a crystallization of Western foreign policy priorities amidst the uncertainties of the post–Cold War era. Criteria for valid intervention in humanitarian crises are yet to be defined by individual governments, let alone by intergovernmental organizations. The appropriate roles for military forces in complex emergencies—a key element in government policy, a major interlocutor for humanitarian actors, and a focus of news attention—has yet to be clarified, much less codified, for either unilateral or multilateral settings. While some form of humanitarian response to many crises seems inevitable, the levels of international involvement and of the resources to be committed remain unclear. Decisions follow in an ad hoc fashion; selective and inconsistent action can be expected.

We are still in a time of transition. The end of the Cold War was a major movement of tectonic plates and the aftershocks continue to be felt.
—UN Secretary-General Boutros Boutros-Ghali[121]

Reflecting governmental attitudes, the levels of political will and of the resources necessary to combat humanitarian crises are likely to fall far short of demand in the years ahead. The uneven results of international initiatives mounted during the early post–Cold War years probably will contribute to a retrenchment. Yet the actual and potential demand grow. One estimate in late 1995 placed the number of states with the potential for civil collapse at no less than eighty.[122] Despite the need for clearer criteria for action and greater cost-effectiveness in the activities mounted, the most likely response of the international community for the time being will be to judge and manage each crisis on a case-by-case basis. For reasons examined earlier, there is greater potential in such a context for media influence on policy debate and outcomes.

Making Better Policy:
Beyond Traditional Interests to Responsibilities

The post–Cold War vacuum in international policy and in retooled institutions provides an occasion for reaffirming time-tested humanitarian principles and finding new ways to enhance their implementation. A redefinition of national interests should take a broader view of the critical importance of a world in which humane values are nurtured, international

The media have the capacity "to educate the public on the new global challenges of human rights and humanitarian crises . . . and to explain why meeting them is in our national interest."
—U.S. Assistant Secretary of State John Shattuck[123]

law respected, and international responsibilities discharged. It is unrealistic to expect governments to make significant bilateral responses to every emergency. However, they may be encouraged, while working together, to devise a more effective institutional apparatus for responding to the most serious incidences of need.

Greater attention to preventive measures is needed. A recurring lesson from the crises reviewed in this study is that prevention would have been more effective—and less expensive—than hurry-up responses to existing emergencies. Since many of these crises occurred in states that had received a substantial amount of development assistance—normally viewed as an investment in crisis prevention—tough questions need to be asked about its failure to forestall conflicts. It may be naive, pointed out a senior government policymaker, to expect that longer-term aid could head off such tensions, but the reduction of aid in the name of budget austerity may end by costing more in the medium and long terms.

Policymakers should take the lead in establishing a more comprehensive and collaborative approach to security, whether through UN or regional institutions, or through bilateral arrangements. They should avoid using aid as a palliative; instead, they should make determined humanitarian action both a component part and an independent element in comprehensive economic and security strategies. Doing so would require concerted use of nongovernmental institutions, including the media.

Early Warning

While the news media may function occasionally as an early warning system, they are no substitute for other systems that monitor and anticipate major humanitarian crises. Often, by the time a crisis is headline news, it has already erupted into violence. The news media offer not so much an early warning system as an imminent alarm signal. Although broader news coverage can flag growing problems in a society, such reporting is too uneven and often too late to be a dependable warning.

Policymakers should have independent and reliable information on the sources of internal conflicts and pending crises. This is the role of government intelligence services—often aided but not supplanted by NGOs and the media. Developments in information technology (in particular the Internet) promise more consistent and comprehensive systems for collection and dissemination of early-warning information.

Policymakers should make more use of the media to educate public opinion on the value of preemptive action, and, since headline news is more concerned with what is than what might be, they should encourage documentary and commentary news to help put across this message.

Containment of Conflict and Peace-Building

The policy challenge in relation to civil wars is to shift from containment to prevention, avoiding the need for face-saving and media-induced placebos, and to support measures for reconstruction. By the time headline news makes the public aware of a crisis, governments are likely to be on the defensive, often using the media to explain or rationalize their own limited or belated actions. Beyond meeting pressures to be seen to be doing something, governments need to confront honestly the inherent limitations of emergency aid-only responses. Comprehensive security and aid programs are required to address complex emergencies. With both global security and economic and social responsibilities, the United Nations is a crucial arena for synchronizing such action, although exercise of the UN's responsibilities in these matters has been remarkably uncreative and ineffective.

Government Accountability to Public Opinion Through the Media

In the United States and the European Union, foreign policy is rarely conducted exclusively by elites behind closed doors. Public opinion matters, whether it runs ahead of or lags behind policy; governments have to maintain a fine balance between leading and reflecting public opinion. Research suggests that the news media, and especially television, increasingly act as the primary source of information for the public about foreign affairs and particularly about the developing world. The media, in effect, provide a common stage for the debate about the new parameters of national and international interests. This is a platform that policymakers should use more assertively.

Government officials would be well-advised to take the media more seriously in the process of policymaking and promotion. "[F]ailure to consider the press aspects of a policy can often mean trouble down the road," observes Martin Lipsky. "A professional attitude toward and sophisticated knowledge of the press creates the opportunity, but only that, for a policymaker to deal with the press—and, yes, to manage relations with the press—so as to better serve the interests of policy goals."[124]

Despite their function of supplying information to the public and spotlighting the actions of governments, the media are unlikely to be in the vanguard of forces promoting the evolution of an international community in which humanitarian principles are paramount and international commitments honored. There are limitations on the contribution that can be expected from an institution geared to domestic audiences and largely focused on the short run. The newly understood importance of prevention, for example, is "inherently nonphotogenic," notes a seasoned humanitarian campaigner.

Government officials should guard against letting either the media or humanitarian actors set or preempt their agenda. Government policy must avoid being either driven or inhibited by public opinion; it should instead use

Peacekeeping operations in particular depend for their support on widespread public awareness of the conflicts and we are committed to doing everything we can to facilitate the work of the media.
—UN Under-Secretary-General Kofi Annan[125]

the media for public education and thereby reduce the need for government management of public opinion in a crisis. The more clearly government policy is articulated, the less policymakers risk overreacting to the media. Policymakers need improved communications strategies to support a leadership role in this regard.

Understanding the Media

More research is needed to understand the complexities of the relationships between the media and policymaking. Most instructive would be a shift from analyzing the role of the media in particular crises to more general findings regarding their effects and potential. State-centric attitudes toward the media regard them as a tool of foreign policy that manipulate political support for or against a decision to intervene in an internal conflict. Humanitarian actors, in contrast, see the media as a powerful champion of human rights, employing their resources with greater regularity to force governments into meeting their respective responsibilities. Post–Cold War experience suggests that consistent policy over time will produce a less radical but more responsible role for the media, particularly in relation to public opinion.

RECOMMENDATIONS FOR HUMANITARIAN AGENCIES

The Future Humanitarian Context

The likely increase in internal armed conflicts during the coming years presents humanitarian agencies with major dilemmas. For example, they stand to win greater backing for their actions to provide emergency assistance as they lose support for the more difficult but ultimately more critical tasks of tackling the root causes of distress and of development education in their own societies. Moreover, as governments lose a taste for security interventions, humanitarian agencies find themselves increasingly in the vanguard of international action, dealing with warring factions that are quickly learning how to manipulate external actors. Media attention to humanitarian activities is also likely to continue its erratic course, with increased or sympathetic coverage by no means guaranteed.

Contributions to Improved Government Policy

The enlarged roles of humanitarian organizations and the expanded expectations of their performance are welcomed by some in these agencies and some in governments, yet caution is in order.

Newly aware of the contributions to humanitarian action that only governments can make, humanitarian actors, spanning as they do governmental, intergovernmental, and nongovernmental institutions, find themselves in a prime position to influence policy. These organizations also form a link between more generalized policymakers and the news media. They often have early, local, and detailed information about potential crises. NGOs in particular have fewer restrictions than governments on sharing such information and are fully able to make extensive use of the media in the process.

However, the range of humanitarian institutions also constitutes its weakness when it comes to influencing government policy. As the preceding analysis suggests, the community of humanitarian organizations often disagrees on the fundamental questions of what it wants from policymakers and which strategies should be pursued to reach that objective. Ambivalence about the necessity for security interventions in support of humanitarian action contributes to a diversity of views about whether and how military and humanitarian actors should work together. Equally divisive is the relative priority accorded to an emergency as contrasted with a longer-term action.

More sustained and effective influence on government policy will require that humanitarian organizations wrestle more energetically with complex policy issues and work harder to identify issues on which consensus may be found. The process of achieving greater clarity on policy objectives also would provide the basis for joint strategies vis-à-vis the media.

Relations with the Media and Public Opinion

For many humanitarian agencies, media relations are dominated by fundraising. Experience demonstrates, however, that the media play many roles that result in humanitarian consequences, only one of which relates to the mobilization of resources. Strategies currently geared to promoting name recognition of individual organizations need therefore to be harmonized with broader and more community-wide objectives in the areas of public education and public policy.

Aid agencies should develop a more sophisticated understanding of the relationship between policy and the media, drawing on the increasing body of research in this area. This in turn would inform communications strategies, which also should take account of the plurality and complexity of the news media as an institution and the possibilities offered by new technologies.[126] Since headline news remains a volatile forum, greater use of documentary and commentary news could stimulate more thoughtful policy debate about complex emergencies in which humanitarian organizations have a strong interest.

There are many well-tested techniques for better relations with the media. Many agencies already have skilled teams exploiting the numerous angles of media coverage; other agencies have yet to acquire those skills. All agencies should do more to coordinate their relations with the media where messages are, or might be, common.

There is no substitute for well-conceived strategies among humanitarian institutions in their interaction with the media. These strategies need to communicate the activities of individual organizations and of the broader family of agencies. Once in place, the strategies will help to guide the resources committed to media relations, both by individual organizations and by the wider family of agencies. Strategies need to become part of the humanitarian culture and to be shared with agency supporters. For practitioners and contributors who place a priority on keeping all expenditures focused on direct assistance to those who suffer, the proposed reorientation will require major changes.

Facilitating the Media's Access to Information

Public opinion research and comments by working journalists alike suggest that humanitarian agencies often overestimate the degree of public and media understanding of their work. The onus is on practitioner organizations to improve the media's access to useful and accurate information about humanitarian mandates and programs. This book reflects the expressed needs of humanitarian organizations to review their interactions with the media, but it is only a first step in a much longer process.

At a practical level, the task of better facilitating the work of the media may be a matter of logistics: for example, of more readily sharing privileged access to conflict zones. Few organizations would question the value of assisting the media to do its job better. In concrete terms, however, taking scarce staff time out to brief journalists or transporting them to where the action is can involve serious trade-offs. For example, should agencies "bump" aid cargo or personnel off flights to make room for news crews? Should agencies spend limited resources to service the needs of itinerate reporters? Such judgments benefit from agency policy that provides supportive general guidelines and that clarifies for donors the approach to be taken.

In a broader sense, facilitating the work of the media involves agency-wide decisions about the extent of resource allocations to be

The most striking trend is perhaps the move by many large agencies to become more open and decentralized, both as organizations, and in particular in their approach to communication, partly in response to increased scrutiny and to calls for greater transparency and accountability, not only to donors but also to beneficiaries.
—UNICEF[127]

made toward media relations. Policy issues also are involved when agencies are forced to weigh the value of publicity for an overlooked cause against their own operational needs. A clear understanding of the potential and the limitations of the media may help humanitarian organizations struggling with these matters.

Understanding the Complexity of the Media

Humanitarian agencies often criticize the media and their perceived shortcomings without understanding the institution's structures and operational constraints. Differentiation within the media by news category and market is essential. For example, CNN, despite recent slippage in audience ratings, remains an effective vehicle for reaching editors globally and policymakers, particularly in the United States, who use it as a kind of 24-hour-a-day wire service. National newspapers can influence policy agendas of the elite; regional papers still have a deep connection with a cross-section of public opinion. In the United States, regional newspapers also syndicate material among themselves, often across regional lines. Since policymakers in the Pentagon and State Department receive a daily digest of all such sources (the "Early Bird"), any particular item of news covered may find its way to the highest level.

Although there is a general need among humanitarian organizations for more skilled media relations, aid agencies should avoid efforts at spin-control and demands for political correctness in reporting on humanitarian topics. They should not expect the media to set an arbitrary balance between "good" and "bad" news in order to reflect a preconceived humanitarian agenda. There always should be an opportunity to put forward an aid agency's particular point of view on a given issue or crisis, but the manipulation of information for short-term gain is counterproductive. In their media relations, agencies should clarify whether they are offering information or opinion. There is no substitute for letting journalists verify events and information for themselves.

Whereas honesty about agency shortcomings is unlikely to result in unfair criticism, attempted manipulation breeds antagonism and cynicism among media professionals. Humanitarian actors who hold that there is no place for amateurs in the humanitarian enterprise should resonate to the desire of journalists to be treated with respect as professionals by aid agencies that understand their tasks and their constraints.

Building Personal Contacts and Preserving Confidentiality

Humanitarian agencies should spend considerable resources developing productive working relationships with journalists. Nurtured over time, these contacts give greater confidence to media professionals, encouraging them to proceed with important stories for which full corroboration is time-consuming or impossible. Personal contacts are equally important with gatekeepers in the system, such as editors and owners. Having trusted contacts in the media world is essential for agencies intent on exposing human rights abuses or advocating serious policy changes.

By virtue of their personal motivations, some journalists may be easier to engage in the humanitarian sphere than others. However, there should be no presumption that the news media are involved for any reason other than to produce objective reporting. There is fierce competition for headline news; agencies should not overlook opinion-page columnists, feature writers, and documentary filmmakers who often have the luxury to consider subjects off the main news radar. A good concerted media strategy, whether of an individual organization or a community of aid groups, will allow for differentiated approaches to media professionals depending on the objectives to be advanced.

Achieving Greater In-depth Coverage

Humanitarian agencies are keen that the media help promote a wider understanding of the root causes of crises. Headline news often reduces complex crises to buzzwords like "chaos" or "anarchy," while overlooking such factors as poverty, repressive regimes, weapons proliferation, and outside interference. In hard-news terms, these factors are difficult to present intelligibly in the space available and often are relegated to more analytical coverage. But agencies cater to this weakness by scripting humanitarian action as a morality play, with victims ("teeming masses of Africans and Asians"), heroes (usually "angels" from the Red Cross or other NGOs), and villains ("local military authorities," "UN bureaucrats," and the like). Simplistic approaches may help raise funds but ultimately work "against the long-term interests of the relief agencies."[128]

Humanitarian agencies could reduce their complicity in stereotypical "formula reporting" by "educating their own workers better," said a journalist renowned for her in-depth reporting of East African crises. They also should provide better briefings for journalists, especially for those departing to an unfolding crisis. There is much room for improvement in what aid organizations do to foster more thoughtful and comprehensive coverage of humanitarian action.

That said, media coverage probably improves only in tandem with greater public education and public demand. Humanitarian agencies should therefore conduct their media relations as part of wider public affairs strategies addressing public education challenges and informing public opinion. Telling the "whole story" also carries risks for humanitarian agencies—already under political fire, greater media scrutiny of aid and its

*S*trategies *for Aid Organizations:*
• Articulate communications strategy. *Each relief organization should publicly articulate its strategy for communicating with the media and the public.*
• Train organization personnel to work with media. *Relief organizations should provide training, particularly for personnel in the field, on how to work with media to improve the timeliness, quality, and accuracy of reporting about developing countries.*
• Evaluate media content. *Relief organizations should evaluate media coverage for accuracy, quality, completeness, timeliness, and professionalism.*
• Create alternative programming. *Relief organizations should work to facilitate documentaries and other programming that provides a more complete image of developing countries.*
• Evaluate relief organization communications. *Many relief organizations—individually and cooperatively—have adopted standards for their communications with the public. All communications activities should be evaluated according to articulated standards.*
—The Annenberg Washington Program[129]

limitations may weaken political and public support of humanitarian missions. But there is no substitute for transparency and accountability. This challenge too has ramifications both for individual agencies and for the wider humanitarian family.

The Costs of Media-Related Functions

As competition for news space has increased, some of the larger humanitarian agencies have begun to pay for the independent production of news or documentary footage to provide broadcasters with a news package. Television networks, though rightly wary of their loss of control over reporting and editing functions, may still utilize prepackaged material if news holes appear and their own products are not available at the time. Partnerships with reliable independent production companies decrease the potential bias and increase the quality of the product and its chances of broadcast or telecast. Given the substantial cost of documentary coverage, however, these undertakings are more feasible for coalitions of organizations than for individual agencies.

Coalitions also have pooled resources to enable joint media relations efforts in recent major crises. A clearly identified point of contact for the media seeking information about a crisis like Rwanda or Somalia has proved a wise investment of funds, as NGO members of InterAction have learned. For its part, the International Council of Voluntary Agencies has placed staff with media and other liaison functions in crises theaters, such as Rwanda and the former Yugoslavia.

Coordination of Purpose and Publicity

The heterogeneity of humanitarian organizations makes it difficult for them to engage the media and public opinion in any concerted way.[130] It is unrealistic and even undesirable for NGOs in particular to organize themselves into a monolithic mouth-piece; however, cacophony and disarray often makes them, in the eyes of the media and policymakers, their own worst enemies. Agencies should devote more time and resources to forging a shared message in various emergencies. The message should go beyond "something must be done," but stop short of getting entangled in complex and divisive political and operational issues.

Coordination of media relations is only one aspect of the challenge of greater interagency collaboration at the planning and operational levels. Coalitions of like-minded NGOs in both Europe and the United States have shown the value of interagency collaboration in the form of enhanced resource mobilization and expanded influence on policymakers and pub-lic opinion. The UN's Department of Humanitarian Affairs has begun to play a role in the coordination of information flows among humanitarian organizations and between them and UN officials, government policymak-ers, and the media. Though news institutions vary in Europe and North America, more could be done by humanitarian organizations to encourage the utilization of available materials on both sides of the Atlantic.

Accountability

There is obviously much room for improvement in the functioning of each of the three sets of institutions comprising the crisis triangle. However, it is humanitarian organizations that have been the most widely faulted and the biggest target of efforts to ensure greater accountability. The welter of agencies flocking to Goma had precedent in the inundation of groups turn-ing up in Jordan while third country nationals fled Kuwait and Iraq in 1990—little has changed since Jordanian authorities described their diffi-culty of distinguishing "the charlatan from the humanitarian."[131]

In highlighting the activities of humanitarian organizations, the media has played a role in encouraging increased effectiveness and greater pro-fessionalism. To date, however, the changes instituted have not improved appreciably the functioning of the system. The desire of governments for greater accountability of UN organizations following their disarray during the crisis in northern Iraq led in 1992 to the creation of the UN Depart-ment of Humanitarian Affairs. DHA has encouraged information-sharing among humanitarian organizations in the UN and beyond, and has been a part of efforts to train practitioners to cope with new challenges. However, fundamental changes have yet to be introduced in the area of coordination or system-wide accountability.

The International Federation of Red Cross and Red Crescent Societies has promoted a useful code of conduct for agencies in disaster response programs, including guidance on information activities. As well as safe-guarding the dignity of victims, the code commits agencies to beware the pitfalls of competition for media coverage. However, in keeping with the voluntary sector ethos of its organizations, the code of conduct is self-policing rather than being backed up by an effective enforcement mecha-nism. Other codes of conduct and sets of principles have been devised and promoted, but with limited appreciable effect.

*W*hile we will cooperate with the media in order to enhance public response, we will not allow external or internal demands for publicity to take prece-dence over the principle of maximising overall relief assistance.

We will avoid competing with other disaster response agencies for media coverage in situations where such coverage may be to the detriment of the service provided to the beneficiaries or to the security of our staff or the beneficiaries.
—IFRC Code of Conduct in Disaster Relief[132]

Given the likelihood of continued major emergencies and of increasing scrutiny of their operations by the media, humanitarian organizations would be well-advised to con-tinue to struggle to find ways and means to upgrade their effectiveness and accountability.

RECOMMENDATIONS FOR THE MEDIA

The Future Context: New Technology and Increased Commercialism

A technological revolution in communications has changed the political landscape. In the words of President Bill Clinton, "Because of a communications revolution, symbolized most clearly by CNN . . . we are front-row history witnesses. We see things as they occur. Now we are impatient if we learn about things an hour after they occur instead of seeing them in the moment."[133] The major advances, how-ever, have not been limited to newsgathering by television. The universal applicability of digital information, the spread of the Internet, and a new level of interactivity in communications are all testing conven-tional wisdom about the ownership and power of information.[134]

The revolution in information technology and the proliferation of news media channels have left commentators divided about future media coverage of foreign affairs.[135] In one assessment, consumers using the new technology are more likely to have access to a greater variety of information sources, allowing them to bypass traditional gatekeepers in the media. "The monolithic empires of mass media are dissolving into an array of cottage in-dustries," Nicholas Negroponte, a commentator on mass communications, has observed.[136] Moreover, an increase in the number of television channels and electronic sources of news information could increase the opportunity for the broadcast and circulation of foreign news. In another assessment, however, there has been a narrowing of the space for "an educated general audience," with the market "now more divided into specialist and tabloid." In the latter view, coverage of foreign news will lose out in the increasingly competitive market to other more powerful and more numerous constituencies.

New technology and newly available news sources notwithstanding, the major television networks are far from obsolete, at least in the United States. At the time of Disney's $19 billion merger with the American Broadcasting Companies, an observer noted that once "[d]ismissed as dinosaurs in a world of ever-expanding information options, broadcast networks and television stations have become the glittering jewels in the media business."[137] Although the networks' share of television audiences has slipped from 90 percent to 60 percent in the last fifteen years, they still possess a decisive hold on viewers and attract the greatest advertising revenue.

There is no firm evidence, however, that technological changes, public demand, or commercial responses will result in the increased capacity being used for foreign coverage. If public demand drops and commercial imperatives follow, foreign news may find itself marginalized in specialized public information broadcasts of the C-span variety. The explosion of "infotainment,"—that is, the packaging of news in an entertainment format—has underscored the upsurge of commercial priorities in the media. Most apparent in the U.S. market, the trend is general and extends well beyond television. Newspapers, described candidly by a U.S. journalist as "a device to deliver consumers to producers," now have finely tuned advertising strategies that affect editorial content and layout decisions. Such developments do not augur well for greater in-depth coverage of foreign affairs in any medium.

The implications of parallel developments in cyberspace are not yet fully clear. Although the Internet promises an unequaled information system for those involved in humanitarian crises, more information does not necessarily bring greater understanding. The main attraction of the Internet is its anarchy and freedom of access, but this attraction may also become its major drawback. Controlling the quality of information on any Internet site takes major resource commitments, as the UN's Department of Humanitarian Affairs discovered while developing Reliefnet. Journalists and editors already have vast information from which to select news. Likewise, policymakers and others with specialized interests will turn to new information services only if they offer faster access to better information.

In summary, there is no conclusive evidence yet that the public is turning away from traditional news sources or local preoccupations. Nor is there any assurance that technological progress will result in improved quantity or quality of media coverage of humanitarian concerns.

The Contribution of the Media to Government Policy

Clarifying the Roles of the Media

Differences persist among and beyond journalists about what is the appropriate role and motivation of the media in influencing government policy. While some profess to be objective reporters without a political agenda, others expect—and some even intend—that their output will produce a policy reaction. The latter perspective was articulated by a U.S. network television reporter who felt that "journalists and NGOs work well together; it is a bonding experience. They go to the same areas for the same reasons: that is, to alleviate suffering." Expressing a more common view, a CNN reporter saw gains in the area of humanitarian action as "a side benefit more than an objective."

Certainly, the dedication of many journalists securing stories of conflict and suffering cannot be doubted. Surveying the casualties suffered by reporters around the world, one report noted that during 1994 at least 72 journalists had been killed, 58 of whom were deliberately targeted, and another 173 were imprisoned.[138] Such journalists are crucial to the improved coverage of conflicts, but over time the perils of the trade may deter coverage.

The newly founded International Center for Humanitarian Reporting (ICHR) in Geneva and its associated journal, *Crosslines Global Report*, are examples of a concerted effort to encourage "humanitarian journalism." Illustrative of the ICHR's practical approach is its initiative in developing a database of global contacts to provide journalists with speedy and reliable sources in war zones.

*O**ur hope is that by becoming better conflict analysts, journalists can become part of the solution rather than part of the problem. Conflict resolution depends upon one's ability to describe conflicts accurately, to identify the problems that generate them, and to evaluate proposed solutions.*
—Richard E. Rubenstein, George Mason University[139]

The extent to which the media, whether as an institution or in the guise of its working professionals, should project themselves as agents of change with an agenda to influence policy remains a much-debated point. Should the media lead or reflect public opinion? As with governmental policymakers, the media have a fine line to tread. One British diplomatic television news editor commented, "Our job is to report, but there is a secondary hope that it will change things, a hope of enlightenment, a hope that this wakes them up in Whitehall." Another journalist confirmed that the optimum media contribution to policy should remain a general rather than a specific one: "to tell the truth, improving understanding and analysis."

Early Warning

Earlier, more consistent, and more probing coverage of potential conflicts, while desirable, is unlikely to become the business of headline news. Early warning remains the primary responsibility of governments and of the United Nations system, although the media may undoubtedly assist, and in certain instances already have, through more comprehensive foreign affairs reporting. To this end, the international media should make better use of aid agencies and local media to follow developments rather than waiting for the herd instinct to direct the attention of the institution toward a particular crisis.

Local Media

Western media should make more use of local journalists to help offset the inadequacies of parachuting outside correspondents into crises. Although there are often problems associated with impartiality of local media in war zones, on the part external support for cash-strapped and independent media institutions in vulnerable countries may contribute not only to improving local journalism but also to conflict prevention.

The issue of "captive" media being used to promote internal conflict needs additional research. In counteracting local propaganda, external media clearly have a crucial role to play, as the earlier discussion of Rwanda indicates. Reaching a local audience remains a major challenge for external media that will require changes in policies as well as practices.

Accountability:
A Responsibility to Report and Educate

Covering Conflicts

The media have a widely acknowledged responsibility to contribute to the education of domestic audiences about the wider threats of complex emergencies, if not through headline news then through other types of coverage. At the same time, however, they are well-advised to retain an independent perspective on humanitarian crises.

This will require keeping their distance from the agendas of both governments and humanitarian organizations, each of which is an important source of information, but each of which also has special interests to promote. Thus, while the temptation is perennial for journalists to produce formulaic accounts of Western humanitarian aid workers and Western diplomats riding to the rescue of distressed populations, the realities of the situation are far more complex and ambiguous.

Retaining an independent perspective will require developing the expertise to evaluate rapidly changing events—and the interpretations given to them by other actors. Foreign-based correspondents with local knowledge are more likely to take an independent view than are news teams parachuted into the middle of a conflict. Although headline news probably will not change formula reporting, documentary and commentary news offer opportunities to explain the domestic relevance of foreign conflicts. The media inevitably will require some time before they are in a position to make their own judgments on the spot in each new crisis, but there is no reason why hard-hitting commentary should wait until the winding down of a relief operation or of media presence.

A subject well within the purview of media attention would involve analysis of why major emergencies sometimes recur in the same setting (for example, Ethiopia), and why they occur in settings that have received ample development assistance over a period of years (e.g., Rwanda and Liberia). The media also have a contribution to make, and a responsibility to make it, in monitoring post-conflict reconstruction, even though policymakers and relief groups may have moved on to the next crisis (as in Haiti). Again, the retrospective role is more likely to be covered in documentary news.

I have made arrangements for the correspondents to take the field . . . and I have suggested to them that they should wear a white uniform to indicate the purity of their character.
—U.S. Civil War Union general Irvin McDowell, quoted by William Howard Russell in *My Diary North and South*[140]

Exercising accountability will require an ability to make discriminating judgments. Unwarranted criticism—of the strategies of donor governments in dealing with warring parties, of the warring parties themselves, and of humanitarian actors—can represent a setback to effective responses. As with the other two major actors in such conflicts, the media will need to balance its responsibility to "tell it like it is" against its need for access and information.

In addition to exercising accountability in relation to other institutions of the crisis triangle, the media should subject itself to higher standards of accountability. As the activities of governments and humanitarian organizations come under greater scrutiny, so, too, will the effects of the media as a humanitarian actor. Certainly the impact of its activities can be profound. The media in general, and television in particular, are well aware of the power of the picture. Not only do the most dramatic pictures dominate headline news but they also can have an impact on other media. The impact on donor publics is palpable.

A television reporter observed that where her BBC team chose to put the satellite link in Bosnia might well affect the deployment of other media, resulting in a concentration of policy attention and humanitarian activities in one area to the detriment of another. Once a satellite link was positioned in Goma, the news flow that it facilitated about refugee distress was massive—in decided contrast to the trickle of news from Kigali during the genocide. As a result, the media contributed to an undesirable imbalance in international activities and resource flows that compounded the difficulties of the new Rwandan regime in the areas of rehabilitation and reconciliation. At a minimum, the media should beware of this danger and take steps to correct imbalances created by picture seduction.

RECOMMENDATIONS FOR THE INSTITUTIONAL TRIANGLE WORKING TOGETHER

A Crisis Mentality and an Ambivalent Public

Among the many elements shared by the institutions of the crisis triangle is the crisis-driven nature of foreign policy, headline news, and humanitarian action. Despite institutional needs, pressures, and cultures that tend to focus minds and resources on the present, all three institutions would benefit from looking further ahead. However great the need for each institution to review individually its performance, doing so together also has special value.

The fact that public opinion waxes hot and cold on humanitarian crises suggests that the process of institutional reflection will need to be sustained by the actors on their own. "Public opinion in matters of foreign policy tends to be shallow, transitory, and lacking in salience" reported a British pollster. In the United Kingdom, he noted, foreign policy rarely features among the top two or three issues polled. Even issues concerning the European Union, he found, are largely regarded as an extension of domestic politics. Public opinion on foreign policy assumes importance only at select times, such as when national troops are deployed or national leaders are playing a high-profile role.

Under these conditions, how should the institutional triangle operate differently to improve international response to humanitarian crises? Overcoming the crisis mentality and stimulating public awareness represent two key challenges.

Cooperation on Media Matters

The most likely common ground for building cooperation within the institutional triangle is more accurate and urgent coverage of headline news, with greater audience impact. Documentary and commentary news will continue to provide the most fertile area of cooperation to address the root causes of complex emergencies—but, however welcome by policymakers and humanitarian organizations, greater depth, continuity, and sophistication will be sought by the media only when their public demands it.

Whatever the state of public awareness, the news media provide one of the few common platforms on which complex emergencies can be debated and undergo arbitration among the various external actors. Governments and humanitarian organizations may resist having a full-fledged public debate on their policies and practices on "opinion pages" or talk shows. In democratic societies, however, that is a major device for articulating interests and hammering out consensus. All institutions can benefit from the town meeting function of the media. The dangers of the perennial short-term focus of governments and aid groups on emergency responses and the absence of strategy to deal with the new world disorder can be highlighted while the media exercises a public service role in the process.

Although each of the three institutions working in civil wars can benefit from greater cooperation, increased contact among them is unlikely to replace the current mistrust and distance with altogether harmonious or synergistic interaction—nor should it. Each set of institutions has and will continue to have its own agendas, constituencies, procedures, mandates, and accountabilities. The media will not cease to play a watchdog role simply because government policymakers and aid officials seek to forge more effective working relationships with them.

At the same time, more collegial working relationships with the media—and a media better informed to understand the complexities of major crises—will improve both policy and action. Benefits of a humanitarian nature also should accrue from the media's potential to move public opinion and power elites at critical moments in the policy process.

The Need for Further Reflection

The issues reviewed in this study are, as indicated throughout, in need of ongoing attention and continuing reflection. This book represents a modest and early step in a longer and arduous process. While a definitive assessment of the nature and extent of influence of the three sets of institutions on one another and on the humanitarian enterprise in general will remain problematic, further experience and analysis should provide better data to understand the interactions more fully.

At this early point in the post–Cold War era, the institutions engaged in policymaking, humanitarian action, and reporting are in ferment. The international community itself is seeking to adapt traditional structures to meet nontraditional challenges. Each set of institutions has launched its own exercises to identify the lessons to be learned from a given crisis or from a series of emergencies. Some of the more successful among such reviews have been those that have enlisted members of all three communities. These exercises often demonstrate the interplay between and among institutions and the extent to which the performance of each influences the success of the others.

A recent example is the newly completed major evaluation of emergency assistance to Rwanda. Undertaken at the initiative of humanitarian organizations that had invested some $1.4 billion in responding to the crisis, the review was managed by a steering committee that mobilized more than $1.7 million to conduct the evaluation. Four separate teams reviewed the historical background, early warning and conflict management, humanitarian aid and effects, and post-war rebuilding. A summary volume highlights individual findings and identifies cross-cutting themes of more general importance. The review concludes, for example, that "The essential failures of the response of the international community were (and continue to be) political."[141] Yet if government decisionmaking were to bear the onus of failure, the media were deeply implicated, particularly in the area of early warning. "The media, with some exceptions, played an irresponsible role in their reporting on Rwanda. The overall failure of the media to accurately and adequately report on a crime against humanity significantly contributed to international disinterest in the genocide, and hence to the inadequate response."[142]

The media, the military, and humanitarian organizations can be the perfect combination, particularly for dealing with large humanitarian disasters, but only if they draw on each other's unique strength and not on the fears and the prejudiced views they sometimes have of each other.
—General Shalikashvili, chairman, Joint Chiefs of Staff[143]

The fact that the most detailed and wide-ranging review of a recent humanitarian crisis has dramatized how much the three sets of institutions influence one another's performance suggests the need for more joint reflection by the members of the crisis triangle. The report also identifies more specific areas for additional research. It observes, for example, that "Significantly, media coverage and its influence upon the operation of a particular humanitarian aid operation has never been subject to rigorous academic analysis."[144]

The Humanitarianism and War initiative itself is an effort that draws on the involvement of all three sets of institutions. Some of those same organizations that participated in the process, which resulted in the present book, intend in the coming months to prepare a more detailed set of guidelines to assist the media and humanitarian organizations in their individual and interactive tasks. This is a pressing task.

Notes

1. For a recent summary see David Hesmondhalgh, "Media Coverage of Humanitarian Emergencies: A Literature Survey," unpublished paper (Department of Media and Communications, Goldsmiths College, London, October 1993). See also Jonathan Benthall, *Disasters, Relief and the Media* (London: Tauris, 1993); Robert I. Rotberg and Thomas G. Weiss (eds.), *From Massacres to Genocide: The Media, Public Policy, and Humanitarian Crises* (Washington: The Brookings Institution and World Peace Foundation, 1996); Edward Girardet (ed.), *Somalia, Rwanda, and Beyond: The Role of International Media in Wars and Humanitarian Crises* (Geneva: Crosslines Global Report, 1995); and Steven Livingston (ed.), *Humanitarian Crises: Meeting the Challenges* (Chicago: Robert R. McCormick Tribune Foundation, 1995).

2. Commission on Global Governance, *Our Global Neighbourhood* (Oxford: Oxford University Press, 1995), 31.

3. See Benthall, *Disasters*, in particular his description of the "Band Aid phenomenon" in 1984, 84–85.

4. Michael Binyon, "Media Tunnel Vision Is Attacked by Hurd," *London Times*, September 10, 1993, 13.

5. As quoted by his spokesperson Sylvana Foa.

6. For a more extended discussion of the policy and programmatic aspects of emergency, rehabilitation, and development assistance, see Larry Minear and Thomas G. Weiss, *Mercy Under Fire: War and the Global Humanitarian Community* (Boulder: Westview, 1995), 28–30. Pages 1–12 also elaborate on the global developments sketched at the beginning of this introduction.

7. For an example of the tensions and convergence between human rights and environmental action, see Aaron Sachs, *Eco-Justice: Linking Human Rights and the Environment* (Washington, D.C.: Worldwatch Institute, 1995). For an extended discussion of tensions between human rights and peacekeeping operations, see Human Rights Watch, *The Lost Agenda: Human Rights and U.N. Field Operations* (New York: Human Rights Watch, 1993).

8. James H. Michel, *Development Co-operation: Efforts and Policies of the Members of the Development Assistance Committee* (Paris: OECD, 1994), 80.

9. Comment by U.S. President Bill Clinton on "A Global Forum," a CNN special broadcast, May 3, 1994.

10. Quoted in William Manchester, *The Last Lion: Winston Spencer Churchill: Alone* (New York: Dell, 1988), 201.

11. Taken from John W. Kingdon, *Agendas, Alternatives, and Public Policies* (New York: Harper/Collins, 1984), 4–5, and Martin Lipsky, *Impact: How the Press Affects Federal Policymaking* (New York: Norton, 1986), 137.

12. Kingdon, *Agendas*, 4.

13. *Ibid.*, 1.

14. For an elaboration of this typology, see Larry Minear and Thomas G. Weiss, *Humanitarian Politics* (New York: Foreign Policy Association, 1995), 32–37.

15. See, for example, Mark Duffield, "Political Action or Humanitarian Action?" in *Rwanda's Disaster Dilemmas Explored* (Geneva: International Federation of Red Cross and Red Crescent Societies, December 1994). See also, Rakiya Omaar and Alex de Waal, *Humanitarianism Unbound?* Discussion Paper No. 5 (London: Africa Rights, 1994).

16. For the most current report, see Michel, *Development Co-operation.*

17. Andrew Natsios, "The Politics of United States Disaster Response," *Mediterranean Quarterly* 6, no. 2 (Spring 1995): 46. If congressional proposals to abolish USAID as a separate entity and integrate its activities more fully into the State Department succeed, the foreign policy connection noted by Natsios would be reinforced.

18. *Ibid.,* 57.

19. On "A Global Forum with President Clinton," CNN, May 3, 1994.

20. See J. Brian Atwood, "Suddenly Chaos," *Washington Post,* July 31, 1994, C9.

21. Remarks by Secretary of Defense William J. Perry to the Fortune 500 Forum, Philadelphia, PA, November 3, 1994.

22. The diagram, prepared by Robert Mansfield, is taken from Larry Minear and Thomas G. Weiss, *Humanitarian Politics* (New York: Foreign Policy Association, 1995), 21; reprinted with permission.

23. For a more extended discussion, see Larry Minear, "Making the Humanitarian System Work Better," in Kevin M. Cahill (ed.), *A Framework for Survival: Health, Human Rights, and Humanitarian Assistance in Conflicts and Disasters* (New York: Council on Foreign Relations, 1993), 234–256.

24. Source: Michel, *Development Co-operation,* 77.

25. See Michel, *Development Co-operation.*

26. *Ibid.,* 2.

27. Steering Committee of the Joint Evaluation of Emergency Assistance to Rwanda, *The International Response to Conflict and Genocide: Lessons from the Rwanda Experience* (Copenhagen: Steering Committee, 1996), 5, Synthesis Report, 70.

28. Michel, *Development Co-operation,* 2.

29. Judith Randel and Tony German (eds.), *The Reality of Aid 1995* (London: Earthscan Publications, 1995), 73. *In The Reality of Aid* series, published each year by a consortium of NGOs with country reports and an analysis of overall aid trends, tends to treat humanitarian issues in ways more tough-minded, critical, and hard-hitting than its DAC counterpart.

30. See Thomas G. Weiss and Leon Gordenher (eds.), *NGOs, the UN, and Global Governance* (Boulder: Lynne Rienner, 1996).

31. For an elaboration of these issues, see Larry Minear and Philippe Guillot, *Soldiers to the Rescue: Humanitarian Lessons from Rwanda* (Paris: OECD, 1996). The volume reviews the activities of international military forces in Rwanda in the context of the growing role of the military around the world in the humanitarian sphere.

32. For a more extended treatment, see Minear and Weiss, *Mercy Under Fire,* 179–195.

33. See "The Future of Aid," *Relief and Rehabilitation Network Newsletter* No. 3 (London: Overseas Development Institute, April 1995), 4–6.

34. For a working definition of coordination, see Larry Minear, et al., *United Nations Coordination of the International Humanitarian Response to the Gulf Crisis 1990–1992* Occasional Paper No. 13 (Providence: Watson Institute, 1992), 3.

35. See *Under the Volcanoes: A World Disasters Report Special Focus on the Rwandan Refugee Crisis* (Geneva: IFRC, 1994).

36. For a review of various coordination arrangements and their results, see Antonio Donini, *The Policies of Mercy: Coordination in Afghanistan, Mozambique, and Rwanda* Occasional Paper No. 22 (Providence: Watson Institute, 1996).

37. Randel and German, *The Reality,* 9.

38. This point is made in an essay by Edward Girardet, "Public Opinion, the Media, and Humanitarianism," in Thomas G. Weiss and Larry Minear (eds.), *Humanitarianism Across Borders: Sustaining Civilians in Times of War* (Boulder: Lynne Rienner, 1993), 39–55.

39. For a useful account of the diverse forces operating in a broadcast news operation, see R. Wallis and S. Baran, *The Known World of Broadcast News: International News and the Electronic Media* (London: Routledge, 1990). The "gatekeeper" notion is used by Steven Livingston, "Suffering in Silence: Media Coverage of War and Famine in the Sudan," in Rotberg and Weiss (eds.), *From Massacres,* 68–89.

40. Carole Zimmerman, "Shifting Focus: The Role of the Media," in *Hunger 1996: Countries in Crisis,* Sixth Annual Report on the State of World Hunger (Silver Spring, MD: Bread for the World Institute, 1995), 54. This chapter (pp. 53–58) is a thoughtful review of the constraints on the media as an agent of education and change in the humanitarian sphere.

41. Herbert J. Gans, *Deciding What's News* (New York: Vintage, 1979).

42. For example, "Impact of Television on U.S. Foreign Policy," Hearing Before the Committee on Foreign Affairs of the House of Representatives, April 26, 1994 (U.S. Government Printing Office, Washington 1994). See also Nik Gowing, *Real-time Television Coverage of Armed Conflicts and Diplomatic Crises: Does It Pressure or Distort Foreign Policy Decisions?* Press, Politics, and Public Policy Working Papers 94-1 (Cambridge: Harvard University, 1994).

43. Summarized by Hesmondhalgh, *Media Coverage.*

44 On one occasion following the Ethiopian famine in the mid-1980s, a delegation of Ethiopians during a visit to Washington to evaluate international response sharply criticized the media, humanitarian organizations, and congressional and administration officials who, they felt, had deprived them of their humanity in their effort to hasten a U.S. response to the crisis.

45. Philip Knightley, *The First Casualty: From the Crimea to Vietnam: The War Correspondent as Hero, Propagandist, and Myth Maker* (New York: Harcourt Brace Jovanovich, 1975), 171.

46. Interview with a U.S. TV network news reporter, December 1, 1994.

47. Gans, *Deciding What's News,* 149, 37.

48. Robert Kaplan, "The Coming Anarchy," *Atlantic Monthly,* February 1994, 44–76.

49. Girardet, "Public Opinion," 46.

50. Gowing, *Real-time Television,* 3–5.

51. For more detail, see Thomas Pakenham, *The Scramble for Africa* (London: Weidenfeld and Nicolson, 1991), 336–338.

52. For an exposition of both models see Steve Livingston and Todd Eachus, "Humanitarian Crises and U.S. Foreign Policy: Somalia and the CNN Effect Reconsidered," *Political Communication* 12, no. 4 (1995): 413–429.

53. Remarks by General Shalikashvili, Chairman of the Joint Chiefs of Staff, to the Robert R. McCormick Tribune Foundation, in Livingston (ed.), *Humanitarian Crises,* 56.

54. See Benthall, *Disasters,* 92–108; as well as Bernard Kouchner and Mario Bettati, *Le devoir d'ingérence: peut-on les laisser mourir?* (Paris: Denoël, 1987).

55. Rony Brauman, "When Suffering Makes a Good Story," in Médecins Sans Frontières, *Life, Death and Aid* (London: Routledge, 1993), 154.

56. Lipsky, *Impact,* 224.

57. For a summary of international response to the Liberia crisis, see Colin Scott, Larry Minear, and Thomas G. Weiss, *Humanitarian Action and Security in Liberia 1989–1994* Occasional Paper No. 21 (Providence: Watson Institute, 1995).

58. UN Consolidated Appeal for Liberia, January 1995, unnumbered DHA document.

59. For an example, see Jeffrey Goldberg, "A War without a Purpose in a Country without Identity," *New York Times Magazine,* January 22, 1995, 36–39.

60. For a graphic account of the importance of external news media to those involved in the conflict, see Lynda Schuster, "The Final Days of Dr. Doe," *Granta* 48 (Summer 1994): 39–95.

61. Sir Anthony Parsons, "Conclusions and Recommendations," in Nigel Rodley (ed.), *To Loose the Bands of Wickedness* (London: Brasey's, 1992), 219.

62. See Steven Livingston, "Suffering in Silence: Media Coverage of War and Suffering in the Sudan," in Robert I. Rotberg and Thomas G. Weiss (eds.), *The Media.*

63. John Prendergast, Center of Concern, interview March 9, 1995.

64. For example, see Karen Hoofer with Don Redding, *Children of Forgotten Emergencies,* a campaign booklet for Save the Children-UK (London, 1995).

65. François Jean (ed.), *Populations in Danger* (London: Libbey, 1992), 65–66.

66. Quoted in Michael R. Beschloss, prepared statement in "Impact of Television on U.S. Foreign Policy," hearing before the Committee on Foreign Affairs of the House of Representatives, 103rd Congress, April 26, 1994, 50. See also Gowing, *Real-time Television Coverage,* 38.

67. Gannett Foundation Media Center, *The Media at War: The Press and the Persian Gulf Conflict* (New York: Gannett Center, 1991), xi.

68. For the wider political context see James Mayall, "Non-intervention, Self-determination, and the New World Order," *International Affairs* no. 67 (July 1991): 421–429.

69. Remarks by General Shalikashvili, Chairman of the Joint Chiefs of Staff, to the Robert R. McCormick Tribune Foundation, in Livingston (ed.), *Humanitarian Crises,* 57.

70. Lee E. Hamilton in "Impact of Television on U.S. Foreign Policy," Congressional hearing, 1.

71. For a detailed tracking of media coverage and policy decisions, see Livingston and Eachus, "Humanitarian Crises," 413–429.

72. John Prendergast, Center of Concern, interview March 9, 1995.

73. See Jean (ed.), *Populations in Danger,* 45–49.

74. Mort Rosenblum, "Lack of Information or Lack of Will?" in Edward R. Girardet (ed.), *Somalia, Rwanda and Beyond: The Role of the International Media in Wars and Humanitarian Crises* (Geneva: Crosslines Global Report, 1995), 79.

75. Interview with former USAID official, December 1994.

76. Rosenblum, "Lack of Information," 79.

77. See Debarati G. Sapir and Hedwig Deconinck, "The Paradox of Humanitarian Assistance and Military Intervention in Somalia," in Thomas G. Weiss (ed.), *The United Nations and Civil Wars* (Boulder: Lynne Rienner, 1995), 151–172.

78. Thomas Keenan, *Back to the Front: Tourisms of War* (Paris: Basse-Normandie, 1994), 143.

, 79. See Andrew Natsios, "Illusions of Influence: The CNN Effect in Complex Emergencies?" in Rotberg and Weiss (eds.), *From Massacres*, 149–168.

80. Lawrence Eagleburger on "Reliable Sources, How Television Shapes Diplomacy," CNN, October 16, 1994.

81. See Warren A. Strobel, *Push Me, Pull You: The News Media, Peace Operations, and US Foreign Policy* (Washington, D.C.: United States Institute of Peace, forthcoming), chapter 4.

82. Donatella Lorch, "Lights, Camera, . . . Land Em," *International Herald-Tribune*, December 10, 1992, 2.

83. Mark Huband, "War Games," *Guardian*, January 9, 1993, 15 (Supplement Section).

84. Rick Lyman, "Occupational Hazards," in Girardet (ed.), *Somalia, Rwanda and Beyond*, 115–128.

85. Quoted in Gowing, *Real-Time Television,* 67. Gowing concludes, the "pictures struck a raw nerve at a time when the administration was uncertain as to whether U.S. troops were still making a valuable contribution to the UN aid mission."

86. *Ibid.,* 27.

87. Frank J. Stech, "Winning CNN Wars," *Parameters* (Autumn 1994): 43.

88. Rosenblum, "Lack of Information," 82.

89. See Thomas G. Weiss, "Collective Spinelessness: U.N. Actions in the Former Yugoslavia," in Richard E. Ullman (ed.), *The World and Yugoslavia's Wars* (New York: Council on Foreign Relations, forthcoming).

90. For a summary of media effect on Bosnia policy, see Warren P. Strobel, "Television Images May Shock but Won't Alter Policy," *Christian Science Monitor*, December 14, 1994, 19.

91. Michael Binyon, "Media Tunnel Vision Is Attacked by Hurd," *London Times*, September 10, 1993, 13.

92. For example, *The Independent* newspaper (UK) throughout 1993.

93. Quoted in Gowing, *Real-time Television,* 72.

94. Quoted in *New York Times,* July 28, 1995, A4.

95. Major General Lewis MacKenzie, "Military Realities of UN Peacekeeping Operations," *RUSI Journal* 138, no. 1 (February 1993): 23.

96. For a discussion of indigenous media roles, see Article 19, International Centre Against Censorship, *Forging War: The Media in Serbia, Croatia and Bosnia-Herzegovina* (Avon: Bath Press, 1994).

97. The observation was made in an interview with the authors by Iain Guest, Fellow at the Refugee Policy Group, Washington D.C. This and other insights on the Haiti crisis were drawn from discussions with Guest and with William G. O'Neill, a consultant to the National Coalition for Haitian Rights.

98. For a summary of the cases for and against U.S. invasion of Haiti, see Robert I. Rotberg, "Give Haiti's Cedras a Deadline for Leaving, Then Act on It," *Christian Science Monitor*, September 12, 1994, 18.

99. Steven Kull and Clay Ramsay, U.S. Public Attitudes on U.S. Involvement in Haiti," Program on International Policy Attitudes, University of Maryland, August 22, 1994.

100. Lawrence A. Pezzullo, "Our Haiti Fiasco," *Washington Post*, May 5, 1994, A23.

101. Remarks by General Shalikashvili, Chairman of the Joint Chiefs of Staff, to the Robert R. McCormick Tribune Foundation, in Livingston (ed.), *Humanitarian Crises*, 5.

102. For a more extended review, see Robert Maguire (team leader), et al., *Haiti Held Hostage: The Quest for Nationhood, 1986–1996* Occasional Paper No. 23 (Providence: Watson Institute, 1996).

103. For an account of media coverage of Burundi-Rwanda 1993–1994, see James MacGuire, "Rwanda before the Massacre," *Forbes Media Critic* 2, no. 1 (Fall 1994): 39.

104. Steering Committee, *International Response*, 2, "Early Warning and Conflict Management," 46.

105. *Ibid.*, "Study 3: Humanitarian Aid and Effects," 150.

106. Thanks to Michael Lally, RTE for this and other insights on the Rwanda crisis.

107. Thomas W. Lippman, "U.S. Troops Withdrawal Ends Frustrating Mission to Save Rwandan Lives," *Washington Post*, October 3, 1994, A11.

108. For a more extended discussion of the positive and negative aspects of *Opération Turquoise* and its putative humanitarian aspects, see Larry Minear and Philippe Guillot, *Soldiers to the Rescue: Humanitarian Lessons from Rwanda* (Paris: OECD, 1996), especially chapter five. The observation about the power of the French presidency was made by Philippe Guillot in an interview with the authors of this book in October 1995.

109. See Steering Committee, *International Response*, 3, 72.

110. "Operation Support Hope 1994," *After Action Review*, chapter 11.

111. For an account of how an experienced regional journalist struggled to understand the ethnic power politics, see Lindsey Hilsum, "Where is Kigali?" *Granta* no. 51 (Autumn 1995): 145–179. Hilsum was reportedly only one of two international journalists in Kigali in early April.

112. The term "media circus" is used in one of the early and more hard-hitting reviews of NGO activities in the crisis, "Rwanda's Disaster Dilemmas Explored," *World Disasters Report* (Geneva: International Federation of Red Cross and Red Crescent Societies, 1995), 13–17.

113. Summarizing a wide-ranging discussion, the formulation of these phases was made by Staffan de Mistura, Director of UNICEF's Division of Public Affairs.

114. Ted Koppel, in "Impact of Television on U.S. Foreign Policy," Congressional hearing, 5. This same line of argument is developed by Natsios, "Illusions of Influence," in Rotberg and Weiss (eds.), *From Massacres*, 149–168. For an account of the degree to which the Clinton administration generally accommodates the media in policymaking, see Bob Woodward, *The Agenda* (New York: Simon and Schuster, 1994), and Lexington, "The Vote Processor," *Economist* 332, no. 7876 (August 13, 1994): 30.

115. See John E. Rielly (ed.), *American Public Opinion and U.S. Foreign Policy 1995* (Chicago: Chicago Council on Foreign Relations, 1995), 31.

116. Mark Duffield, "Complex Emergencies and the Crisis of Developmentalism," *IDS Bulletin: Linking Relief and Development* 25, no. 4 (October 1994): 37–45.

117. Quoted in William Shawcross, "Around the World in Eighty Briefings," *Spectator* 273, no. 8661 (July 9, 1994): 9.

118. See, e.g., Gordon Adam, "Radio's Peacekeeping Potential in Humanitarian Crises," in Girardet (ed.), *Somalia, Rwanda, and Beyond*, 179–190.

119. Raymond Bonner, "Trying to Document Rights Abuses," *New York Times*, July 26, 1995, A10.

120. *International Response to Conflict and Genocide*, 3, "Humanitarian Aid and Effects."

121. Boutros Boutros-Ghali, *Supplement to an Agenda for Peace*, document A/50/60, S/1995/1, January 3, 1995, para. 5.

122. Catherine Toups, "Mitchell Heads New Unit for Averting World Crises," *Washington Times*, November 17, 1995, 16.

123. John Shattuck, "Human Rights and Humanitarian Crises: Policy-Making and the Media," in Rotberg and Weiss (eds.), *From Massacres*, 175.

124. Lipsky, *Impact*, 217.

125. Quoted in Roger Cohen, "In Bosnia, the War That Can't Be Seen," *New York Times*, December 25, 1994, E4.

126. A number of NGOs, including the Mennonite Central Committee, already have development strategies and train their headquarters and overseas staff accordingly.

127. Anne Winter, *Communication for Development in an International Context: A Review of its Current Status, Emerging Trends, and the Potential for Cooperative Activities between Agencies and with External Partners* (Geneva: UNICEF, 1995), 6.

128. John C. Hammock and Joel R. Charny, "Emergency Responses as Morality Play: The Media, the Relief Agencies, and the Need for Capacity Building," in Rotberg and Weiss (eds.), *From Massacres,* 115–135.

129. Fred H. Cate (ed.), *International Disaster Communications: Harnessing the Power of Communications to Avert Disasters and Save Lives* (Washington, D.C.: The Annenberg Washington Program in Communications Policy Studies of Northwestern University, 1994), 59–60.

130. See Winter, "Communication," 18–19.

131. Minear et al., *United Nations Coordination,* 35.

132. International Federation of Red Cross and Red Crescent Societies, *World Disasters Report 1994*, (Geneva: IFRC, 1994), 26–32.

133. On "A Global Forum with President Clinton," CNN, May 3, 1994.

134. For a discussion, see "Part One: Capitalizing on Technology and Sustaining Media Attention," in Rotberg and Weiss (eds.), *From Massacres*, 14–89.

135. For a comprehensive assessment of future trends, see W. Russell Neuman, *The Future of the Mass Audience* (Cambridge: Cambridge University Press, 1991).

136. Nicholas Negroponte, *Being Digital* (New York: Knopf, 1995), 57.

137. Paul Fahri, "Disney Co. and CapCities/ABC Agree to a $19 Billion Merger," *Washington Post*, August 1, 1995, A16.

138. Edward Girardet (ed.), "Record Number of Journalists Killed in 1994," *Crosslines Global Report*, March 1995, 43–46.

139. Richard E. Rubenstein, *Frameworks for Interpreting Conflict: A Handbook for Journalists* (Fairfax, Virginia: George Mason University, 1994), 121.

140. Knightley, *The First Casualty*, 19.

141. See Steering Committee, *International Response* 5, "Synthesis Report," 11.

142. *Ibid.*, 2, 10.

143. Remarks by General Shalikashvili, Chairman of the Joint Chiefs of Staff, to the Robert R. McCormick Tribune Foundation, in Livingston (ed.), *Humanitarian Crises*, 58.

144. Steering Committee, *International Response* 3, 151.

Acronyms

ACUNS	Academic Council on the United Nations System
AID	Agency for International Development [USA]
BBC	British Broadcasting Corporation
CNN	Cable News Network
CRS	Catholic Relief Services
DAC	Development Assistance Committee [OECD]
DHA	Department of Humanitarian Affairs [UN]
DPA	Department of Political Affairs [UN]
DPKO	Department of Peace-keeping Operations [UN]
EC	European Community
ECHO	European Union [formerly Community] Humanitarian Office
ECOMOG	Economic Community Monitoring Group [ECOWAS]
ECOSOC	Economic and Social Council [UN]
ECOWAS	Economic Community of West African States
EU	European Union
ESCAP	Economic Commission for Asia and the Pacific
FAO	Food and Agriculture Organization [UN]
IASC	Inter-Agency Standing Committee [UN]
ICHR	International Centre for Humanitarian Reporting
ICRC	International Committee of the Red Cross
ICVA	International Council of Voluntary Agencies
IFOR	Implementation Force [former Yugoslavia]
IFRC	International Federation of Red Cross and Red Crescent Societies
IGO	intergovernmental organization
IMF	International Monetary Fund
IOM	International Organization for Migration
ITN	Independent Television News [UK]
LWF	Lutheran World Federation
MSF	Médecins Sans Frontières (Doctors Without Borders)
NATO	North Atlantic Treaty Organization
NGO	nongovernmental organization
OAU	Organization of African Unity
ODA	official development assistance

ODA [UK]	Overseas Development Administration [UK]
OECD	Organisation for Economic Co-operation and Development
OFDA	Office of Foreign Disaster Assistance [USA]
ONUSAL	United Nations Observer Mission in El Salvador
PDD	Presidential Decision Directive
PVO	private voluntary organization
SPLA	Sudan People's Liberation Army
SRSG	Special Representative of the UN Secretary-General
UNAMIR	United Nations Assistance Mission in Rwanda
UNCDF	United Nations Capital Development Fund
UNDP	United Nations Development Programme
UNDRO	United Nations Disaster Relief Office
UNESCO	United Nations Educational, Scientific and Cultural Organization
UNFPA	United Nations Fund for Population Activities
UNHCR	United Nations High Commissioner for Refugees
UNICEF	United Nations Children's Fund
UNITAF	Unified Task Force [Somalia]
UNOMIL	United Nations Observer Mission in Liberia
UNOSOM	United Nations Operation in Somalia
UNPA	United Nations Protected Area [former Yugoslavia]
UNPROFOR	United Nations Protection Force [former Yugoslavia]
UNV	United Nations Volunteers
USAID	United States Agency for International Development
VOLAG	voluntary agency
WFP	World Food Programme
WHO	World Health Organization

Glossary

Civil war An intrastate armed conflict

Complex emergencies Internal political crises and/or armed conflicts complicated by an array of political, social, and economic factors

Donors External actors committing resources to humanitarian action, normally governments or groups of governments acting through governmental, intergovernmental, or nongovernmental channels

Emergency aid Life-saving humanitarian relief—normally food, shelter, and medical care

Humanitarian action The provision of emergency aid and the protection of basic human rights

Humanitarian intervention Nonconsensual humanitarian activities mounted from outside an area in crisis, sometimes involving the threat or the use of military force

Impartiality The relief of suffering according to need without regard to such factors as nationality, race, religion, politics, or ideology

Media The broad range of Western news media, except where otherwise defined

Neutrality The avoidance of taking sides in hostilities or political conflict

Peacekeeping The interposition of neutral troops between or among warring factors with their consent to observe and monitor a cease-fire or other peace agreement

Peace enforcement The imposition of external military force to achieve peace or to advance other objectives against the wishes or without the consent of the warring factions

Selected Bibliography

Carol Belamy, *The State of the World's Children 1996* (New York: Oxford University Press, 1996).

Jonathan Benthall, *Disasters, Relief and the Media* (London: I.B. Tauris, 1993).

Fred H. Cate (ed.), *International Disaster Communications: Harnessing the Power of Communications to Avert Disasters and Save Lives* (Washington, D.C.: The Annenberg Washington Program in Communications Policy Studies of Northwestern University, 1994).

Mark Duffield, "Complex Emergencies and the Crisis of Developmentalism," *IDS Bulletin: Linking Relief and Development* 25: 4 (October 1994): 37–45.

James Fallows, *Breaking the News: How the Media Undermine American Democracy* (New York: Pantheon Books, 1996).

Freedom Forum Media Studies Center, *The Media and Foreign Policy in the Post–Cold War World* (New York: Columbia University, 1993).

Herbert J. Gans, *Deciding What's News* (New York: Vintage, 1979).

Edward Girardet (ed.), *Somalia, Rwanda, and Beyond: The Role of the International Media in Wars and Humanitarian Crises* (Geneva: Crosslines Global Report, 1995).

Nik Gowing, *Real-time Television Coverage of Armed Conflicts and Diplomatic Crises: Does It Pressure or Distort Foreign Policy Decisions?* Press, Politics, and Public Policy Working Papers 94-1 (Cambridge: Harvard, 1994).

John W. Kingdon, *Agendas, Alternatives, and Public Policies* (New York: Harper/Collins, 1984).

Phillip Knightly, *The First Casualty: From the Crimea to Vietnam: The War Correspondent as Hero, Propagandist, and Myth Maker* (New York: Harcourt Brace Jovanovich, 1975).

Martin Lipsky, *Impact: How the Press Affects Federal Policymaking* (New York: Norton, 1986).

Steven Livingston (ed.), *Humanitarian Crises: Meeting the Challenges* (Chicago: Robert R. McCormick Tribune Foundation, 1995).

Larry Minear and Thomas G. Weiss, *Humanitarian Politics* (New York: Foreign Policy Association, 1995).

———, *Mercy Under Fire: War and the Global Humanitarian Community* (Boulder: Westview, 1995).

Johanna Neuman, *Lights, Camera, War* (New York: St. Martin's Press, 1996).

W. Russell Neuman, *The Future of the Mass Audience* (Cambridge: Cambridge University Press, 1991).

Rakiya Omaar and Alex de Waal, *Humanitarianism Unbound? Current Dilemmas Facing Multi-Mandate Relief Operations in Political Emergencies,* Discussion Paper No. 5 (London: Africa Rights, 1994).

Robert I. Rotberg and Thomas G. Weiss (eds.), *From Massacres to Genocide: The Media, Public Policy, and Humanitarian Crises* (Washington: The Brookings Institution and World Peace Foundation, 1996).

Richard E. Rubenstein, et al., *Frameworks for Interpreting Conflict: A Handbook for Journalists* (Fairfax, Virginia: George Mason University, 1994).

Warren P. Strobel, *Push Me, Pull You: The News Media, Peace Operations, and US Foreign Policy* (Washington, D.C.: United States Institute of Peace, forthcoming).

Thomas G. Weiss (ed.), *The United Nations and Civil Wars* (Boulder: Lynne Rienner, 1995).

Thomas G. Weiss and Leon Gordenker (eds.), *NGOs, the UN, and Global Governance* (Boulder: Lynne Rienner, 1996).

United Nations High Commissioner for Refugees, *The State of the World's Refugees 1995: In Search of Solutions* (New York: Oxford University Press, 1995).

"What in the World Is Going On?" *Crosslines Global Report, The Independent Newsjournal on Humanitarian Action, Development and World Trends* 3: 2 (April-May 1995).

Anne Winter, *Communication for Development in an International Context: A Review of its Current Status, Emerging Trends, and the Potential for Co-operative Activities between Agencies and with External Partners*, (Geneva: UNICEF, 1995).

About the Authors and
— Media Workshops Participants —

Larry Minear has worked on humanitarian and development issues since 1972 as a NGO official and consultant to UN organizations and governments. In 1990, he headed an international team that carried out a case study of Operation Lifeline Sudan. With Thomas G. Weiss, he has co-directed the Humanitarianism and War Project since 1991 and serves as its principal researcher.

Colin Scott, a policy and communications consultant based in Washington, D.C., serves as a consultant to the Humanitarianism and War Project. He spent seven years with Save the Children (UK), including three years as senior press officer and two years managing its programs in Mali, Liberia, and Sierra Leone. Previously he worked in media relations in British NGOs and local government.

Thomas G. Weiss is associate director of the Thomas J. Watson Jr. Institute for International Studies and executive director of the Academic Council on the United Nations System. He previously held a number of posts at the United Nations and the International Peace Academy. He has written extensively on development, peacekeeping, humanitarian relief, and international organizations.

David Anable: Chair, Journalism Department, College of
    Communication, Boston University
Andrew Bearpark: Head of Emergency Aid, Overseas Development
    Administration
Charles Bierbauer: Senior Washington Correspondent, CNN
Lincoln P. Bloomfield: Professor of Political Science, Massachusetts
    Institute of Technology
Janet Breslin: Department of National Security Policy and Strategy,
    National War College
Tom Callahan: Foreign Relations Committee, U.S. Senate
Fred Cate: Professor of Law, Indiana University

Nick Cater: Words & Pictures
Ted Clark: National Public Radio
John Coonrod: Director, The Hunger Project
Jeff Danziger: Political Cartoonist, *The Christian Science Monitor*
Kathleen deLaski: Deputy to Under Secretary of Defense for Policy
     Liaison, Office of the U.S. Secretary of Defense, The Pentagon
Staffan de Mistura: Director, Division of Public Affairs, UNICEF
Alain Destexhe, M.D.: Sénateur, Belgium Parliament
George Devendorf: Assistant Program Officer, Foreign Disaster
     Assistance, InterAction
Bo Elding: Senior Advisor, Swedish International Development Agency
Dennis Gallagher: Executive Director, Refugee Policy Group
William Garvelink: Deputy Director, Office of Foreign Disaster
     Assistance, U.S. Agency for International Development
Pierre Gassmann: Head, Press Division, International Committee of the
     Red Cross
Arlene Getz: Correspondent, Gemini News Service
Edward Girardet: Editor, *Crosslines Global Report*, International Centre
     for Humanitarian Reporting
Nik Gowing: Diplomatic Editor, Channel Four News, UK
Stephen G. Greene: Senior Editor, *The Chronicle of Philanthropy*
Martin Griffiths: Director, UNDHA
John Hammock: President, Oxfam America
Ann Hannum: Program Associate, World Peace Foundation
Henny Helmich: Director, External Cooperation of the OECD
     Development Centre
Lori Hendricks: Special Assistant, Africa Region, U.S. Department of
     Defense, The Pentagon
Lindsey Hilsum: Freelance Journalist
Brennon Jones: Former Executive Director, InterPress Third World News
     Agency
Mehr Kahn: Director, Division of Information, UNICEF
Steven Livingston: National Center for Communication Studies, George
     Washington University
Elizabeth Lukasavich: External Resources Coordinator, Office of Foreign
     Disaster Assistance, U.S. Agency for International Development
Emily MacFarquhar: Correspondent, *U.S. News and World Report*
Richard Melanson: National War College
Bhaskar Menon: Editor, *International Documents Review*
Andrew Natsios: Executive Director, World Vision Relief and
     Development
Johanna Neuman: Foreign Editor, *USA Today*

Robert Nevitt: Department of National Security Policy and Strategy, National War College

Kathleen Newland: Senior Associate, Carnegie Endowment for International Peace

Benjamin Pogrund: Editor, *World Times*

Lionel Rosenblatt: President, Refugees International

Robert I. Rotberg: President, World Peace Foundation

Charles Royer: Director, Institute of Politics, Kennedy School of Government, Harvard University

Randolph Ryan: Staff Reporter, *The Boston Globe*

John Shattuck: Assistant Secretary of State for Human Rights and Humanitarian Affairs

Peter Shiras: Director, Government Relations and Public Outreach, InterAction

Ann Stingle: International Communication Associate, Corporate Communication, American Red Cross

Paul Tooher: Foreign Editor, *Providence Journal-Bulletin*

Richard Ullman: Professor of Politics, Woodrow Wilson School, Princeton University

Peter Walker: Director, Disaster and Refugee Policy Division, International Federation of Red Cross and Red Crescent Societies

Ruth Walker: Editorial Editor, *The Christian Science Monitor*

Melissa Wells: U.S. Ambassador; Fellow, Center for International Affairs, Harvard University

Robert White: Associate Editor, *Minneapolis Star Tribune*

Index

The Thomas J. Watson Jr. Institute
for International Studies,
Brown University, and the
— Humanitarianism and War Project —

Brown University's Thomas J. Watson Jr. Institute for International Studies was established in 1986 to promote the work of students, faculty, visiting scholars, and policy practitioners who are committed to analyzing global problems and developing initiatives that address them. The Watson Institute promotes research, teaching, and public education on international affairs, an area of inquiry that encompasses interstate relations; transnational, regional, and global phenomena; and cross-national, comparative studies.

The Watson Institute supports and coordinates the activities of scholars and practitioners with interdisciplinary approaches to contemporary global problems. Most are social scientists working on political, economic, social, or cultural issues, along with scholars from the humanities and the natural sciences whose perspectives contribute directly to the understanding of these issues. The Watson Institute's affiliated centers and programs currently engage in a broad range of activities, from improving the teaching of international studies to contributing to research and public education about international security, the comparative study of development, health, hunger, the United Nations, U.S. foreign policy, and issues arising within Africa, the Americas, Asia, Europe, the Middle East, and the former Soviet Union.

* * *

Day in and day out, from Yugoslavia to Somalia, Chechnya to Rwanda, Angola to Haiti, civil strife inflicts widespread human suffering. Even where bloodshed has abated, as in Cambodia, El Salvador, and Mozambique, tensions and the awesome task of rebuilding war-torn countries remain.

How can the international community better protect those caught in national and regional conflicts? How can it more effectively assist nations to turn the corner on violence and become productive societies? Can aid

120

become an effective force for the resolution of conflicts? Must humanitarian action await the request of warring parties or, with the ebbing of East-West tensions, can humane values form the new cornerstone of international relations?

These questions are addressed by the Watson Institute's Humanitarianism and War Project. The applied research and policy initiative is an effort by an independent team of researchers based at Brown University and drawing on the expertise of scholars and practitioners from around the world to assist the international community to chart its course in the post–Cold War era. The codirectors of the Project are Thomas G. Weiss, Associate Director of the Watson Institute and Executive Director of the Academic Council on the United Nations System; and Larry Minear, Senior Fellow at the Watson Institute and the Project's principal researcher.

During the first phase (1991–1993), the Project was cosponsored by the Refugee Policy Group (Washington, DC), and support was provided by two dozen practitioner organizations and interested foundations. These included four governments (Netherlands, United Kingdom, United States, and France); six intergovernmental organizations (UNICEF, WFP, UNHCR, UNDP, DHA/UNDRO, and the UN Special Program for the Horn of Africa); ten nongovernmental organizations (Catholic Relief Services, Danish Refugee Council, the International Centre for Human Rights and Democratic Development [Canada], International Federation of Red Cross and Red Crescent Societies, Lutheran World Federation, Lutheran World Relief, Mennonite Central Committee, Norwegian Refugee Council, Oxfam-UK, and Save the Children Fund-UK); and three foundations (Pew Charitable Trusts, Rockefeller Foundation, and Arias Foundation).

During its second phase (1994–1996), the Project has been based at the Watson Institute and has financial support to date from: four governments (Australia, Netherlands, United Kingdom, and the United States); eight intergovernmental organizations (UNICEF, UNDP, UN Volunteers, UN University, International Organization for Migration, OECD Development Centre, European Commission Humanitarian Office, and the Department of Humanitarian Affairs); seventeen nongovernmental organizations (American Red Cross, Catholic Relief Services, Danish Refugee Council, International Federation of Red Cross and Red Crescent Societies, International Orthodox Christian Charities, International Rescue Committee, Lutheran World Federation, Lutheran World Relief, Mennonite Central Committee, Nordic Red Cross Societies [Finnish, Icelandic, Norwegian & Swedish], Norwegian Refugee Council, Save the Children-US, World Vision, and Trócaire); and three foundations (Pew Charitable Trusts, McKnight Foundation, and U.S. Institute of Peace).

The Project has conducted field research in the Horn of Africa, the Persian Gulf, Central America, Cambodia, the former Yugoslavia, Liberia,

Rwanda, Georgia, and Haiti in order to publish a series of case studies and policy recommendations. In addition to journal articles and op-ed pieces, the Project has also published four books: *Mercy Under Fire: War and the Global Humanitarian Community* (1995); *Humanitarian Politics* (1995); *Humanitarian Action in Times of War: A Handbook for Practitioners* (1993, available in English, Spanish, and French); and a volume of collected essays by practitioners, *Humanitarianism Across Borders: Sustaining Civilians in Times of War* (1993). The Project has also prepared a training module which is currently in use by UN organizations.

The Project will carry out additional field research in Chechnya and Nagorno-Karabakh; complete a guide entitled *The News Media, Civil War, and Humanitarian Action*; review the humanitarian and political impacts of economic sanctions; share findings and recommendations in conferences and training events; and continue an extensive array of publications. The Project regularly publishes progress reports. These reports and additional information are available on the internet at:

http://www.brown.edu/Departments/Watson_Institute/H_W/H_W_ms.shtml

About the Book

The civil wars—and ensuing humanitarian crises—that have been prominent features of the first post–Cold War decade have revealed interactions among a triangle of institutions: the news media, governments, and humanitarian organizations. This three-way relationship has elicited considerable commentary, with the media often depicted as a decisive causal link between a given crisis and how governments and aid groups behave. Beyond loose talk of the "CNN factor," however, analysis of the linkages and attention to their implications have been lacking.

This brief volume looks at institutional interactions between the news media (both print and electronic) on the one hand, and government policymakers and humanitarian agencies on the other. Case studies from Liberia, northern Iraq, Somalia, the former Yugoslavia, Haiti, and Rwanda distill some of the experiences gained from calamities that have elicited widely varying coverage and responses.

Acknowledging that the three sets of actors have differing agendas, limitations, and constituencies, the book nevertheless identifies a common interest in improving the quality of interactions for the benefit of victims.

Frontline Diplomacy:
Humanitarian Aid and Conflict in Africa

John Prendergast

Prendergast investigates the negative impacts of humanitarian aid in conflict situations and explores how these can be minimized and how aid might instead contribute to conflict prevention and peace building.

Rebuilding Societies After Civil War:
Critical Roles for International Assistance

edited by Krishna Kumar

This collection addresses questions fundamental to international aid to war-torn societies. Drawing on case studies, the authors focus particularly on issues of food security, health services, human rights, military demobilization, resettlement, and reconciliation at the local level.

Humanitarian Action in Times of War:
A Handbook for Practitioners

Larry Minear *and* Thomas G. Weiss

"I would rank the Handbook among the top three most useful resource manuals on the market today." —*Studies in Conflict and Terrorism*

ISBN 1-55587-676-5

9 781555 876760   90000>